FARSI (PERSIAN)
FOR BEGINNERS

DEDICATION

For Sofia, my daughter living in three worlds. May you be the link: logos, pathos, and mythos.

ACKNOWLEDGMENT

I would like to express my gratitude to many people who helped me with this book. My sister Ameneh (Maliheh) Atoofi who patiently and meticulously proofread the manuscript many times, provided me with valuable advice on contents, and organized many other aspects such as photos and sound files. Of course, I am indebted to other members of my family for the creation of this book, some with their wonderful photographic skills (Donya and Majid), and others with the sound files and advice (Nahid, Haydeh, Homyra, Davood, Mehran, Baran, Bahareh, Majid, Donya, Diba, Banafsheh, Azadeh, and Marjan). I also want to thank my wonderful niece, Zahra (Ghazaleh) Shoai, who helped me with the addition of the new vocabulary terms. I have been very fortunate to be around wonderful people who constantly encouraged me and gave me moral support in this project: my soulmate Viviana, my daughter, Sofia, and my best of friends and family, Marjan Shokri and Alireza Keshvari. I would also like to thank my editors and reviewers, Terri Jadick, Sandra Korinchak, Robert Goforth, and Nancy Goh from Tuttle Publishing for their wonderful comments, suggestions, and guidance. It has been great learning from the masters.

Learning Conversational Farsi

FARSI (PERSIAN)
FOR BEGINNERS
SECOND EDITION

Saeid Atoofi, Ph.D.
Content Advisor:
Maliheh (Ameneh) Atoofi

TUTTLE Publishing

Tokyo | Rutland, Vermont | Singapore

"Books to Span the East and West"

Tuttle Publishing was founded in 1832 in the small New England town of Rutland, Vermont [USA]. Our core values remain as strong today as they were then—to publish best-in-class books which bring people together one page at a time. In 1948, we established a publishing outpost in Japan—and Tuttle is now a leader in publishing English-language books about the arts, languages and cultures of Asia. The world has become a much smaller place today and Asia's economic and cultural influence has grown. Yet the need for meaningful dialogue and information about this diverse region has never been greater. Over the past seven decades, Tuttle has published thousands of books on subjects ranging from martial arts and paper crafts to language learning and literature—and our talented authors, illustrators, designers and photographers have won many prestigious awards. We welcome you to explore the wealth of information available on Asia at **www.tuttlepublishing.com**.

Published by Tuttle Publishing, an imprint of Periplus Editions (HK) Ltd.

www.tuttlepublishing.com

Library of Congress Control Number: 2015940721

ISBN 978-0-8048-5439-9 *(Previously published as ISBN 978-0-8048-4182-5)*

Distributed by

North America,
Latin America & Europe
Tuttle Publishing
364 Innovation Drive
North Clarendon,
VT 05759-9436 U.S.A.
Tel: 1 (802) 773-8930
Fax: 1 (802) 773-6993
info@tuttlepublishing.com
www.tuttlepublishing.com

Japan
Tuttle Publishing
Yaekari Building, 3rd Floor,
5-4-12 Osaki
Shinagawa-ku, Tokyo 141 0032
Tel: (81) 3 5437-0171
Fax: (81) 3 5437-0755
sales@tuttle.co.jp
www.tuttle.co.jp

Asia Pacific
Berkeley Books Pte. Ltd.
3 Kallang Sector #04-01,
Singapore 349278
Tel: (65) 6741-2178
Fax: (65) 6741-2179
inquiries@periplus.com.sg
www.tuttlepublishing.com

Second Edition 2020
First Edition 2015
26 25 24 23   6 5 4 3   2311VP
Printed in Malaysia

TUTTLE PUBLISHING® is a registered trademark of Tuttle Publishing, a division of Periplus Editions (HK) Ltd.

Contents

The Audio Recordings may also be Downloaded.

How to Download the Audio Recordings of this Book.
1. You must have an internet connection.
2. Type the URL below into to your web browser.

https://www.tuttlepublishing.com/farsi-persian-for-beginners-2

For support email us at info@tuttlepublishing.com.

To the Learner

Farsi shekar ast (Farsi is sugar). This is how Farsi speakers refer to their own language, because they believe speaking Farsi is a sweet treat to the tongue. I hope this book provides you a sweet first step to learning Farsi. This book will teach you how to:

- Read and write all Farsi letters

- Combine letters to write words in Farsi

- Read and write simple sentences or phrases in Farsi

- Greet someone, interact at a bank, get a taxi, invite someone to a party, and many other useful conversational skills

- Become aware of the differences between colloquial and formal forms of Farsi, and the context in which each form is used

- Express yourself as native Farsi speakers would do, adjusting your speech according to culturally relevant situations

- Learn essential Farsi grammar in the context of daily conversation

- Read some proverbs, songs, and poems in Farsi

- Scan Farsi content in newspapers, emails, or websites to get the gist of what is being discussed

Get ready! In *Farsi for Beginners*, I will help you step by step to learn, and enjoy essential Farsi.

Introduction

Whatever has motivated you to learn Farsi, there is probably no better time to learn this vibrant and rich language than today. Iran is home to a great number of classical and contemporary poets, philosophers, and artists who have written and created most of their works in Farsi. Knowing Farsi will allow you to enjoy the poems of Rumi and Hafiz, read the philosophical works of Nasir Khusraw and Allameh Tabatabaei, and watch the world-class cinema of Kiarostami and Farhadi in their original language.

Farsi for Beginners is intended as an entry level to learning Farsi. You do not need to have any prior background knowledge in Farsi to start using this book. However, "entry level" does not mean simple or limited. The contents of this book have been devised to reflect real use of language by ordinary people in the streets of Tehran. At the same time, the chapters are very much accessible to novice learners. And, although beginners in Farsi will get the most out of this book, the chapters can still be challenging for intermediate and advanced learners of Farsi because they provide ample new vocabulary words and are rich in cultural information.

Its accessibility sets this book apart from other Farsi language books. For the most part, learning Farsi as a second language has been out of reach for general audiences. Most Farsi instructional books are written in a highly specialized language, or focus on specific language skills, or lack the freshness of current approaches to learning a second language. Too often, learners using those books need to stomach tedious grammar instructions chapter after chapter, or will learn only one skill (for instance, how to read Farsi script). But not here!

Learning a new script can be very intimidating for new language learners. Most Farsi books either avoid teaching the alphabet altogether by using a romanized version of the Farsi words throughout, or they show the entire alphabet on the first few pages and assume that the reader will be able to remember the sounds of all the 32 Farsi letters at one time, immediately knowing how complex words should be pronounced by connecting these letters.

I wrote *Farsi for Beginners* with the perspective of a new language learner in mind. Throughout the book, I have provided sufficient transition stages so that you can comfortably learn each language skill, step by step. For instance, you can start reading Farsi conversations using recognizable transliterations, while at the same time learning four or five Farsi letters. As you move on to the next chapter, the study of the previous Farsi letters is reinforced, and gradually the transliterations are replaced by Farsi letters and words.

I also wanted to make learning Farsi fun and useful. All chapters are based on a fictional story following a mixed Iranian and American family visiting Iran. You get to know each character of the story while they take a cab, shop, exchange money, and receive an invitation for a family dinner. Again, I had the reader in mind. I imagined what kind of skills and knowledge a new Farsi learner would need to accomplish real and culturally relevant tasks. What kind of interactions would he or she have, with whom, where, and how?

However, making this book useful and fun did not come at the expense of forgetting to teach you the structures of the Farsi language. Every chapter contains practical grammar sections that directly link to the contents of the conversation you encounter in that chapter. As such, you will learn Farsi grammar and vocabulary in the context of real situations, some of which will require you to bend or break "textbook" grammar rules. For instance, just like most languages of the world, in Farsi there is not just one way to greet everyone. So, based on the person and place, you will learn different greetings that require you to become more formal or less formal, use contractions, and even change your pronunciation.

This book also adapts a modern pedagogical approach to learning language. Situations, conversations, grammar structures, and the pronunciation are authentic. They are not simplified or toned down. A simplified language is an artificial language that no one uses in the real world. Modern methods of language learning also acknowledge that language and culture are inseparable aspects of communication. You will learn relevant Farsi vocabulary and grammar in the context of the cultural background that accompanies them. For instance, in Iran you have to insist to pay the fare to a taxi driver although he or she may seem to refuse to take your money in your first attempt, a concept called **tarof kardan**.

I enjoyed writing this book and I hope you find it valuable and informative. Language learning is a lifelong endeavor. When you are done with this book, keep going. Read, watch, listen, and chat, text, e-mail and blog in Farsi. I strongly believe that language is more than a medium in which to communicate. When you learn a new language, little by little, you start to see and experience the world from the perspective of the speakers of that language. And my wish is that this can bring us all closer to one another.

How to Use This Book

Farsi may be enjoyable to learn, but it does take effort! To get the most from your work, the best approach is to study a chapter in a single day, and then repeat the same chapter the following day, before moving onto the next chapter. The chapters are rather long, and it may not be possible for everyone to dedicate enough time to cover one complete chapter a day. In that case, I suggest working through a chapter on two or three successive days without taking a break between days. If you need to take a day off during your Farsi study, try to do it between two chapters and not within a chapter.

Learning a language, for the most part, is a motor skill similar to riding a bike. A language is not a piece of information that is learned, but a skill that is *acquired*. Reading instructions about how to ride a bike does not teach you to ride one. Rather, you learn to ride a bike by the pedaling, falling, and then more pedaling. Do not be afraid to make mistakes. More importantly, do not limit yourself to reading the conversations in the chapters or practicing the Farsi letters only once. Repeat the chapters! Every now and then, go back to previous chapters and repeat some of the pronunciation and writing practices. Your tongue, your vocal cords, and the muscles of your fingers are doing most of the learning. Give them enough opportunity to acquire the language.

The book provides detailed instructions in each section. However, here are some general pointers that will help you best use the book.

■ Most sections for which you will need help with pronunciation are marked with an audio disc icon like this: 🎧 . Listen to the correct pronunciation before you start that section of the book. When in doubt, go back to the audio to listen to the specific sound you are unsure about, and repeat it out loud.

■ Sometimes transliterations include accent marks. These accents have been used to facilitate your correct pronunciation of Farsi words. For instance "ā" stands for the long form of this vowel in Farsi, which is the sound of "a" in the English word "tall." This is in contrast to the short sound of "a" in Farsi, which is pronounced like the "a" in the English word "man."

■ Unlike English, Farsi is a formal language. There are many ways in which Farsi grammar is influenced by the level of formality people feel that they need to use with their audience. While studying the Conversations, pay attention to subtle differences in the use of pronouns, contraction of verbs, and changes in pronunciation.

■ Due to the high level of differences between formal and informal language in Farsi, the chapters include two additional aids for learners. First, in the Conversations, informal variants of words (i.e., colloquial words) have been marked with an asterisk like this: *. Second, right after each Conversation, there is a table showing all the colloquial words which were used. The table includes their formal variants as well as their actual meanings in Farsi. When you see an asterisk next to a word, go to the table and study the formal version of the word.

■ All chapters include a section called *Let's Talk*. Practice the provided examples many times—not just once. Imagine yourself in a real situation in which you have to use the example. Be creative. For instance, as you practice the example, replace a pronoun with a name, or switch verbs.

■ For letter-writing practice, line guides are provided on the page to facilitate your initial learning process. As you become more proficient, try to avoid using the line guides and practice on plain paper.

■ Language is learned both from the bottom-up and from the top-down. While you need the letters to compose words, at the same time, you can also learn words and complete sentences without the need to deconstruct them into their single letters. As you progress through the book, you will find that whole English words have been replaced by their Farsi counterparts because you had encountered the Farsi term before, either in the same chapter or previous chapters. So, while you try to combine letters and make sense of the sound of a word, also try to get a feeling for the overall look of the word and try to capture it in your mind as a whole. When in doubt, look back at the Vocabulary list.

■ An Answer Key to the practice activities is found at the end of the book. But be careful! Instead of jumping right to the Answer Key whenever you find yourself stumped, just respond to all the questions as best you can, and only then review your responses against the provided answers.

Some considerations

■ There are many dialects of Farsi. Apart from Dari and Tajiki, two languages very closely related to Farsi used primarily in Afghanistan and Tajikistan, there are a great number of different dialects and accents within Iran. This book for the most part teaches the Tehrani dialect and intonation style, primarily used by people residing in Iran's capital, Tehran. Due to heavy use of this dialect on national TV and radio stations, people of other regions in Iran understand and may even be able to speak this dialect with ease. (However, the reverse is not always true. That is, people from Tehran may find it somewhat difficult to understand people from elsewhere in Iran.) Hence, even though it is only one among many Farsi dialects, knowing the Tehrani dialect will allow you to reach a greater audience.

■ As mentioned in the Introduction, romanized versions of the Farsi, or transliterations, have been provided for English speakers who want to learn Farsi. As such, the transliterations are only intended to facilitate the pronunciation of Farsi words; they are *not* meant to provide comparable phonetic notations between Farsi and English letters. So, you may encounter times when some of the letters in Farsi have been transliterated differently in different words. For instance, you may find the letter **heh** ه at the end of Farsi words transliterated as **e**, **eh**, and sometimes **a**, a reflection of its varying pronunciations. Use the accompanied audio disc when you are not sure about a certain pronunciation.

■ As you will see in the chapters, in Farsi writing, there are three short vowels which are generally not written, but are pronounced. Hence, the reader has to guess the sound of these vowels by recognizing the whole word rather than breaking down the word into its vowels and consonants. Some Farsi instructional books use diacritics for the missing vowels to jump-start new learners. I chose not to use this method for pedagogical reasons. Although in the beginning it may be a bit more difficult to read a Farsi word in this book, later you will come to appreciate not having had the aid of those diacritics, for two good reasons. First, in real life, nobody uses these diacritics. You will never find a real Farsi book, magazine, or Internet site that uses them on words. So, if you were to rely on these aids, later you would come to a complete stop at the point when you needed to switch to real use of real language. Second, as I mentioned previously, language learning is both a bottom-up and a top-down process. New learners, of course, need to know the letters in order to read and write words in a new language (a bottom-up process). However, and at the same time, beginners have to be guided to see the larger picture—words and phrases. Avoiding the use of diacritics, as we do in *Farsi for Beginners*, encourages you toward a global (top-down) view of language that facilitates a natural and uninterrupted way of reading.

Transliteration Conventions

In order to facilitate independent reading, transliterations have been used to help new Farsi learners get an idea on how to pronounce the words and sentences in this book. Transliteration can never replace actual pronunciation of utterances. Use the accompanied audio disc when you are not sure about a certain pronunciation. Also, transliteration is only a convention. That is, while the transliteration system used in this book is very consistent, other Farsi instructional materials may choose different methods to transcribe the sound of words. Finally, transliterations are meant to provide comparable phonetic notations between Farsi and English phonemes (the sound of letters). So, you may encounter times when some of the Farsi letters have been transliterated differently in different words as a reflection of its varying pronunciations.

Transliteration	Sound and example (based on English sounds)
a	"a" as in "bad"
ā	"a" as in "tall"
b	"b" as in "boy"
p	"p" as in "pen"
t	"t" as in "tree"
s	"s" as in "sand"
j	"j" as in "jam"
ch	"ch" as in "China"
h	"h" as in "home"
kh	"j" in "Jaime," as pronounced in Spanish
d	"d" as in "dog"
z	"z" as in "zoo"
r	"r" as in "rich"
zh	"g" as in "general," as pronounced in French

Transliteration	Sound and example (based on English sounds)
sh	"sh" as in "short"
gh	"r" in "Rome," as pronounced in French
f	"f" as in "fan"
c	"c" as in "cat"
g	"g" as in "good"
l	"l" as in "language"
m	"m" as in "mother"
n	"n" as in "nice"
o	"o" as in "home"
oo	"oo" as in "pool"
e	"e" as in "bed"
i	"i" as in "bid"
ee	"ee" as in "been"
eh	"et" as in "gourmet"

Farsi Scripts

There are 32 letters in the Farsi alphabet. Farsi is written in script, in that most letters connect to other letters. These letters have four forms which are called initial, medial, final, and independent. There are seven letters which never connect to any subsequent letter. These letters have only two forms. In each chapter you will learn part of the Farsi alphabet in more details. You will have plenty of time and ways to practice the letters in each form and within words. However, if you are a type of learner who prefers to know the alphabet before starting to learn words and sentences, you can study the following table to get acquainted with the Farsi alphabet system first.

Name of the letter	Letter position			
	final	middle	initial	independent
alef	ﺎ			ا
be	ﺐ	ﺒ	ﺑ	ب
pe	ﭗ	ﭙ	ﭘ	پ
te	ﺖ	ﺘ	ﺗ	ت
se	ﺚ	ﺜ	ﺛ	ث
jim	ﺞ	ﺠ	ﺟ	ج
che	ﭻ	ﭽ	ﭼ	چ
he	ﺢ	ﺤ	ﺣ	ح
khe	ﺦ	ﺨ	ﺧ	خ
dāl	ﺪ			د
zāl	ﺬ			ذ
re	ﺮ			ر

Name of the letter	Letter position			
	final	middle	initial	independent
ze	ـز			ز
zhe	ـژ			ژ
sin	ـس	ـسـ	سـ	س
shin	ـش	ـشـ	شـ	ش
sād	ـص	ـصـ	صـ	ص
zād	ـض	ـضـ	ضـ	ض
tā	ـط	ـطـ	ط	ط
zā	ـظ	ـظـ	ظ	ظ
eyn	ـع	ـعـ	عـ	ع
gheyn	ـغ	ـغـ	غـ	غ
fe	ـف	ـفـ	فـ	ف
ghāf	ـق	ـقـ	قـ	ق
kāf	ـک	ـکـ	کـ	ک
gāf	ـگ	ـگـ	گـ	گ
lām	ـل	ـلـ	لـ	ل
mim	ـم	ـمـ	مـ	م
nun	ـن	ـنـ	نـ	ن
vāv	ـو			و
he	ـه	ـهـ	هـ	ه
ye	ـی	ـیـ	یـ	ی

Salām va ahvālporsi
سلام و احوال پرسی
Greetings

In this chapter, you will learn the customs of greetings in Iranian culture. You will also learn some Farsi letters and also become familiar with how to conjugate the verb *(to be)* **boodan** بودن.

1.1 Conversation

[01 día]

Didār bā rahmatihā
دیدار با رحمتی ها
Meeting the Rahmatis

Daniel Paradise is traveling to Iran with his Iranian wife, Nasrin Rahmati, and their child, Sara, to visit his wife's family in Iran and to do some sightseeing. Nasrin's parents and their son, Farzad, have come to the airport to welcome them. Listen to the conversation first. Then replay the audio, this time reading along with the text below.

NASRIN:	**Salām māmān joon***. *Hello my dear Mama.*	سلام مامان جون*.
MRS. RAHMATI:	**Salām dokhtaram.** *Hello my daughter.*	سلام دخترم.
NASRIN:	**Delam barāt* tang shodeh bood.** *I missed you.* (Literally: "My heart had become narrow for you.")	دلم برات* تنگ شده بود.
NASRIN:	**Bābā koo? Farzād kojāst?** *Where is Daddy? Where is Farzad?*	بابا کو؟ فرزاد کجاست*؟
MRS. RAHMATI:	**Ānhā dārand miānd***. *They're coming.*	آنها دارند میاند*.
NASRIN:	**In Dānieleh***. *This is Daniel.*	این دانیله*.
MRS. RAHMATI:	**Salām. Hāle shomā khoob ast?** *Hello. How are you?*	سلام. حال شما خوب است؟
DANIEL:	**Man khoobam***. *I'm well.*	من خوبم*.

MRS. RAHMATI: **In Sārāeh*?** *Is this Sara?*	این سارائه*؟
NASRIN: **Āreh, fārsi harf mizaneh*.** *Yes, she speaks Farsi.*	آره، فارسی حرف میزنه*.
MRS. RHAMATI: **Ghorboonet* beram Sārā joon.** *I adore you, dear Sara. (Literally: "I die for you, dear Sara.")*	قربونت برم* سارا جون.
SARA: **Salām, mādar bozorg.** *Hello, Grandma.*	سلام مادر بزرگ.

[01sect2]

1.2 Formal vs. Colloquial: Words from the Conversation

As explained in the Introduction, the following table provides alternative forms of formal and colloquial words used in the Conversation. The colloquial forms (محاوره ای **mohāverei**) have been marked with an asterisk (*). While reading the Conversation, consider the context in which a colloquial word has been used (usually denoting a very close relationship, or that the conversational partners are of the same age). Then, study the formal forms (رسمی **rasmi**) to become familiar with the way you would speak to a person formally, or would find that word in printed materials, for example, in a Farsi book or a newspaper.

Formal	رسمی	Colloquial*	محاوره ای*	Meaning
māmān jān	مامان جان	māmān joon	مامان جون	*dear Mom*
barāye to	برای تو	barāt	برات	*for you*
kojā ast?	کجا است؟	kojāst?	کجاست؟	*Where is it/he/she?*
miāyand	می‌آیند	miānd	میاند	*they come*
Dāniel ast?	دانیال است؟	Dānieleh?	دانیاله؟	*Is [this] Daniel?*
khoob hastam	خوب هستم	khoobam	خوبم	*I am good*
Sārā hast?	سارا هست؟	Sārāeh?	سارائه؟	*Is [this] Sara?*
harf mizanad	حرف می‌زند	harf mizaneh	حرف میزنه	*speaks*
ghorbāne to beravam	قربان تو بروم	ghorboonet beram	قربونت برم	*I adore you/* *I would die for you*

1.3 Let's Talk

[01sect3]

In Farsi, there is a class of pronouns that attach themselves to a noun and very often make these nouns possessive. These are the endings to use for different persons.

Person	Singular		Plural	
1st	-am	م	-emān	مان
2nd	-at	ت	-etān	تان
3rd	-ash, -esh	ش	-eshān	شان

For instance, in the Conversation, Mrs. Rahmati told her daughter, Nasrin, **Salām dokhta-ram** سلام دخترم (*Hello, my daughter*). Here **-am** م functions as *my* in English. Accordingly, if she wanted to say *your daughter*, then she would say, **dokhtar**at دخترت. And, for *their daughter*, she would say **dokhtar**eshān دخترشان.

Like other languages, there are a variety of ways in which you can ask "How are you?" in Farsi. Mrs. Rahmati used a very formal way of presenting this question to Daniel, whom she was seeing for the first time, by saying, **Hāle shomā khoob ast?** حال شما خوب است؟.

Here are other ways of asking "How are you?" in different contexts:

Context	Transliteration	Farsi	Meaning
With a stranger or an older person	**shomā khoobid?**	شما خوبید؟	*Are you* (formal) *well?*
	khoob hastid?	خوب هستید؟	*Are you* (formal) *well?*
	khoobid?	خوبید؟	*Are you* (formal) *well?*
	chetor hastid?	چطور هستید؟	*How are you* (formal)?
With a friend or same age relative	**khoob hasti?**	خوب هستی؟	*Are you* (informal) *well?*
	khoobi?	خوبی؟	*Are you* (informal) *well?*
	chetori?	چطوری؟	*How are you* (informal)?

■ Try It

Now let's practice a bit with what you have learned so far. Imagine you are greeting people in different situations. Read and repeat to yourself the following sentences. The letters in shade show the bound pronouns. Can you recognize which person they refer to?

a. **Dokhtar**at **khobeh?** دخترت خوبه؟
    Is your daughter well? (Very informal, used among close friends)

b. **Pesar**etān **khobeh?** پسرتان خوبه؟
    Is your son well? (Formal, used to show respect toward an older person)

c. **Bābāhāy**etān **khoob hastand?** باباهایتان خوب هستند؟
    Are your fathers well? (Formal, one probably would use this in formal writings)

d. **Mādar bozorg**esh **chetoreh?** مادربزرگش چطوره؟
    How's his/her grandma? (Informal, used among friends)

e. **Hāleh māmān o bāb**at **khoobeh?** حال مامان و بابات خوبه؟
    Are your mom and dad well? (Informal, used among friends)

f. **Chetori Farzād?** چطوری فرزاد؟
    How are you, Farzad? (Informal, used among friends)

■ The Farsi Alphabet

Farsi is written from right to left. There are 32 letters in the Farsi alphabet. Farsi is written in script, in that most letters connect to other letters. Of the 32 letters, 25 connect to both the previous and subsequent letters. These letters have four forms which are called initial, medial, final, and independent. There are seven letters which never connect to any subsequent letter. These letters have only two forms, initial, and final.

Don't be intimidated in thinking that you cannot learn so many forms of letters. As you will see in this chapter as well as in the subsequent chapters, different forms of each letter look very similar, so they are easy to recognize. And also, there is a specific pattern for how different forms of the letters are written. Let's start by learning a few of these letters.

1.4 The Letters *Alef, Lām, Sin,* and *Mim*

[01 sect4]

■ The letter alef ا or آ

The letter **alef** is one of those letters which only connects to letters preceding it, and not following it. If **alef** is the first letter in a word, then it stands alone. As such, **alef** has only two forms, an initial form for when it begins a word, and a final form for when there is another letter prior to it. **Alef** can be pronounced in two main ways in Farsi. First, like the short "a" in the English word "m**a**n." Second, as a Farsi long "ā," like in the English word "t**a**ll."

Here are the forms for **alef** with a short "a":

Position	Form	As in	Pronounced	Meaning
Initial	ا	است	ast	*is*
Final	ـا	بابا	bābā	*father*

The **alef** with a long ā is called **ā bā kollāh** ("the ā with the hat"). While its initial form is an **alef** with a line above it, its final form is the same as a normal **alef**.

Position	Form	As in	Pronounced	Meaning
Initial	آ	آره	āreh	*yes*
Final	ﻞ	مادر	**mādar**	*mother*
Independent	ا	سارا	**Sārā**	*Sara*

Let's practice writing the letter **alef** on the following lines. Don't forget to write from right to left!

Now, let's learn some more of Farsi letters. At this point, we are mostly concerned with the shapes and sounds of the letters. While you are reading this section, remember to:

1. Pay attention to the forms of each letter as it is written in different places in a word. At least one part of each letter will remain unchanged regardless of the form.
2. Write the different forms of the letters on the lines provided.
3. Listen to the audio for the pronunciation of each word in the following tables. Then replay the audio, this time reading along with the words.

■ The letter lām ل

The letter **lām** is pronounced like the "l" in the English word "language." The following table shows the different forms of the letter **lām** ل. Learn the letter, practice the pronunciation, and remember the meaning of each word.

Position	Form	As in	Pronounced	Meaning
Initial	ـل	لب	l**ab**	*lips*
Medial	ـلـ	قلب	gha**l**b	*heart*
Final	ـل	گل	go**l**	*flower*
Independent	ل	پول	poo**l**	*money*
Lām followed by **alef**	لا or ـلا	سلام	sal**ā**m	*hello*

Now practice writing the four forms of the letter **lām** ل.

■ The letter mim مـ

The letter **mim** مـ is pronounced like the "m" in the English word "mother." The following table shows the four forms of the letter **mim** مـ. Learn the letter, practice the pronunciation, and remember the meaning of each word.

Position	Form	As in	Pronounced	Meaning
Initial	مـ	من	man	*I*
Medial	ـمـ	بمن	beman	*to me*
Final	ـم	دلم	delam	*my heart*
Independent	م	سلام	salām	*hello*

Now practice writing the four forms of the letter **mim** مـ.

■ The letter sin س

The letter **sin** س is pronounced like the "s" in the English name "Sam." The following table shows the four forms of the letter **sin** س. Learn the letter, practice the pronunciation, and remember the meaning of each word.

Position	Form	As in	Pronounced	Meaning
Initial	ــســ	سلام	salām	*hello*
Medial	ـسـ	پسر	pesar	*boy/son*
Final	ـس	حس	hes	*sense*
Independent	س	ترس	tars	*fear*

Now practice writing the letter **sin** س in its four forms.

1.5 Let's Write

Now let's learn how to connect the letters you have learned thus far together in order to form words. For example, if we want to connect **alef** ا and **sin** س in that order, **alef** uses its initial form and **sin** uses its independent form, giving us اس, because **alef** does not connect to the letter that comes after it, and as **sin** is the last letter. However, if we reverse the order, then **sin** uses its initial form and **alef** uses its final form, giving us سا.

In the following exercise, reproduce the different combinations of the letters **alef**, **lām**, and **sin**. Writing Farsi words over and over is the best way to learn and remember the way words are written, so that your Farsi writing skills become strong. Note that the following words may not have any particular meanings. We just want you to learn the ways Farsi letters are combined together.

	Order of letters	Independent forms	As words
1	alef + lām + sin	س ل ا	الس
2	alef + sin + lām	ل س ا	اسل
3	lām + sin + alef	ا س ل	لسا
4	lām + alef + sin	س ا ل	لاس
5	sin + lām + alef	ا ل س	سلا
6	sin + alef + lām	ل ا س	سال

If you remember, when **lām** is followed by **alef**, as in the case of numbers 4 and 5, the letters take the forms لا or ﻼ.

1.6 Cultural Insight

Delam barāt tang shodeh bood   دلم برات تنگ شده بود
I missed you. (Literally: "My heart had become narrow for you.")

Farsi is riddled with emotional expressions which may seem like hyperbole to outsiders. For instance, Farsi speakers frequently use the word **jān** جان or its informal form **joon** جون (translated literally as "life force" or "soul") toward one another to display intima-

cy and closeness. Most phone calls, letters, and emails to friends, relatives, and acquaintances open with the name of the receiver plus the word **jān** جان, for example, **Sara jān** سارا جان (literally: "my life, Sara").

In the Conversation section, Nasrin used many expressions to show emotional closeness to her mother. First, she used the word **joon** جون in the phrase **Salām māmān joon** سلام مامان جون (*Hello, dear Mama*) to greet her mother. Later, she told her mother **Delam barāt tang shodeh bood** دلم برات تنگ شده بود (literally: "My heart had become narrow for you") to convey that she had missed her mother, Mrs. Rahmati. Similarly, Mrs. Rahmati used the expression **Ghorboonet beram Sārā joon** قربونت برم سارا جون (literally: "I would die for you, dear Sara") to express that she was very excited to see her granddaughter. In Farsi, these expressions are used frequently among intimates to display endearment and show affection, especially among females.

1.7 Vocabulary

[01sect7]

In this section, read the words in Farsi and memorize their meanings. Then play back the audio and check your pronunciation. You can use this section for a reference if you have a question about the meaning of the words in the Conversation section.

Transliteration	Farsi	Meaning
salām	سلام	*hello*
mādar/māmān	مادر\مامان	*mother/mommy*
jān/joon	جان\جون	*dear*
dokhtar	دختر	*daughter*

Transliteration	Farsi	Meaning
del	دل	*heart*
tang/del tang shodan	تنگ\دل تنگ شدن	*tight/narrow/to miss someone*
pedar/bābā	پدر\بابا	*father/daddy*
ānhā	آنها	*they*
kojā/koo	کجا\کو	*where*
in	این	*this*
hāle shomā chetoreh?	حال شما چطوره؟	*how are you?*
shomā	شما	*you* (formal)
khoob	خب\خوب	*well/good*
man	من	*I*
āreh	آره	*yes*
harf-zadan	حرف زدن	*to speak*
mādar bozorg	مادر بزرگ	*grandma*

1.8 Grammar Point: The verb (*to be*) boodan

While reading the Conversation, you might have wondered why the counterpart of the English verb "is" in Farsi (**ast** است) had different forms in different places. For instance, when Nasrin introduced her husband to her mom, she said, **In Dāniel**eh این دانیله (*This is Daniel*). In another place, Nasrin asked her mom, **Farzād koj**āst? فرزاد کجاست؟ (*Where is Farzad?*).

Like English, Farsi also uses both full and contracted forms of the verb to be. In English, we can say, "I am happy," "Jane is beautiful," and "You are smart," or we can contract the verb and say, "I'm happy," "Jane's beautiful," and "You're smart." In the same way, Nasrin used contracted forms of the *be*-verb.

Like most Indo-European languages, Farsi verbs are conjugated. Conjugation means that speakers attach endings to verbs that provide information about the person, number, and tense of a verb. In Farsi, very often pronouns are omitted from sentences because the verb endings imply the pronoun.

The following table shows the present tense conjugation of the full and contracted forms of the verb **boodan** (*to be*).

Full/Contracted form	Example	
hastam/am (*I am*)	**khoob hastam/khoobam** (*I am well.*)	خوب هستم\خوبم
hasti/i (*you are*)	**Dāniel hasti/Dānieli?** (*Are you Daniel?*)	دانیل هستی\دانیلی؟
hast/ast/eh (*he/she/it is*)	**Kojā hast/kojāst/kojāeh?** (*Where is he/she/it?*)	کجا هست\کجاست\کجائه؟
hastim/im (*we are*)	**Del tang hastim/del tangim** (*We are heavy-hearted*)	دل تنگ هستیم\دلتنگیم
hastid/id (*you all are*)	**Chetor hastid/chetorid?** (*How are you?*)	چطور هستید؟\چطورید؟
hastand/and (*they are*)	**Ānhā khāneh hastand/** **ānha khāneānd** (*They are home*)	آنها خانه هستند\آنها خانه اند

boodan (*to be*)		
English	**Farsi**	**Example**
I am	**hastam**	**khoob hastam** خوب هستم (*I am well.*)

Hast is the present tense stem of the verb **boodan**. The endings -am, -i, -im, -id, and -and have been added to the stem to include information about different persons and numbers. Remember these endings, because this is all you need to know to conjugate nearly all Farsi verbs in the present tense.

You may have also noticed that the third person singular form of the verb **boodan** has two contracted forms, -ast and -eh. Unlike English, Farsi does not have a gender marking for the third person, such as *he*, *she*, and *it*, and as such, the difference between **hast** and -ast is not of the gender of the speaker. **Hast** is often used to emphasize the existence of something.

1.9 Poem
[01sect9]

When Muslim Arabs conquered the Persian Empire in 644 AD, many words of Arabic origin found their way into Farsi. In fact, modern Farsi script is an adaptation of the Arabic script. One of the greatest Persian poets, Ferdowsi (935–1020 AD) is famous for his exclusive use of Farsi (i.e., non-Arabic) words in his poetry. His great epic is called *Shahnameh* ("The Book of the Kings"). Most school textbooks in Iran start with the following poem from Ferdowsi.

Tavanā bovad harke dānā bovad
Ze dānesh dele pir bornā bovad

توانا بود هرکه دانا بود
ز دانش دل پیر برنا بود

The wise person is also an able person
From wisdom an old heart turns to young

1.10 Exercises

1. How many letters are there in the Farsi alphabet?

2. What are the four forms of the Farsi letters? Write all the forms for the letter **sin**.

3. What do the words **Dāniel joon** دانیال جون mean?

4. Draw lines on a piece of paper and copy the following letters several times. Make sure you write the letters exactly the same way as below.

5. Connect the following letters to create words, then write down their transliterations. Remember that the letter **alef** can only connect to the previous and not the following letter.

Example:

mā   مـا = ا + م

a. _____ م + س

b. _____ ل + م

c. _____ ل + ا

d. _____ س + ا + ل

e. _____ م + ل + س

f. _____ م + ا + ل

6. How do you say "How are you?" in Farsi, both formally and informally?

_____

_____

7. Translate the following sentences from English into Farsi using transliteration. Refer to the Conversation and Vocabulary sections to find the right translation for each Farsi word.

Example:

Hi Daddy.   **Salām bābā.**

a. Where is mother?   _____

b. Dear grandmother   _____

c. Is this Daniel? _____

d. My daughter speaks Farsi. _____

e. Daniel and Sara are coming. _____

Haml-o naghl
حمل و نقل
Transportation

In this chapter, we will learn more new letters, and discuss personal and possessive pronouns in Farsi. We will also familiarize ourselves with some of the cultural issues regarding transportation in Iran.

2.1 Conversation

[02dia]

Dar tāxi
در تاکسی
In the taxi

Listen to the conversation first. Then replay the audio, this time reading along with the text below. In this chapter, the Paradise family takes a cab from the airport to their hotel in the northern part of Tehran.

DANIEL:	**Nasrin az oon* tāxi bepors.** *Nasrin, ask that taxi.*	نسرین از اون* تاکسی بپرس.
NASRIN:	**Āghā in tāxi khālieh*?** *Sir, is this taxi available? (Literally: "Is this taxi empty?")*	آقا این تاکسی خالیه*؟
DRIVER:	**Baleh khānoom, biāeed bālā.** *Yes ma'am, get in. (Literally: "Come up.")*	بله خانم، بیایید بالا.
NASRIN:	**Sārā jān, to dar rā bāz kon.** *Dear Sara, open the door.*	سارا جان، تو در را باز کن.
SARA:	**Māmān man dastam bandeh*.** *My hands are full.*	مامان من دستم بنده*.
DRIVER:	**Shomā kojā mirid*?** *Where are you going?*	شما کجا میرید*؟
NASRIN:	**Mā rā be hotel Homā bebareed.** *Take us to Hotel Homa.*	ما را به هتل هما ببرید.

(Some time later, the Paradise family reaches their destination)

DANIEL:	**Merci mā injā piādeh mishim.***	مرسی ما این جا پیاده میشیم.*
	Thank you. We'll get out here.	
NASRIN:	**Che ghadr taghdim konam?**	چه قدر تقدیم کنم؟
	How much can I offer you?	
DRIVER:	**Befarmāeed, ghābel nadāreh***.	بفرمایید، قابل نداره.*
	Please, it's not worth mentioning.	
NASRIN:	**Khāhesh mikonam, befarmāeed.**	خواهش می‌کنم، بفرمایید.
	Please, tell me.	
DRIVER:	**Si hezār toman misheh***.	سی هزار تومن میشه.*
	It's thirty thousand tomans.	
NASRIN:	**Dāniel to pool dāri?**	دانیل، تو پول داری؟
	Daniel, do you have the money?	
DANIEL:	**Anām ham be oo bedam***?	انعام هم به او بدم*؟
	Should I give him a tip?	
NASRIN:	**Agar doost dāri.**	اگر دوست داری.
	If you like.	
DANIEL:	**Khedmate shomā.**	خدمت شما.
	Here you are.	
DRIVER:	**Merci, be shomā khosh begozarad.**	مرسی، به شما خوش بگذرد.
	Thank you. Have a nice stay.	
DANIEL:	**Khodāhāfez.**	خداحافظ.
	Goodbye.	

2.2 Formal vs. Colloquial: Words from the Conversation
[02sect2]

The colloquial forms of the words (محاوره ای **mohāverei**) in the Conversation have been marked with an asterisk (*). While reading the conversation, consider the context in which a colloquial word has been used. Then, study the formal forms (رسمی **rasmi**) to become familiar with the way you would address a person formally, or would find that word in a Farsi book or a newspaper.

Formal	رسمی	Colloquial*	محاوره ای *	Meaning
ān	آن	oon	اون	*that*
khāli ast	خالی است	khālieh	خالیه	*is empty*
band ast	بند است	bandeh	بنده	*is full/tied up*
miravid	می روید	mirid	میرید	*you go (pl.)*
piādeh mishavim	پیاده می شویم	piādeh mishim	پیاده میشیم	*we will get out*
ghābel nadārad	قابل ندارد	ghābel nadāreh	قابل نداره	*It is not worth mentioning*
mishavad	می شود	misheh	میشه	*will become*
bedaham	بدهم	bedam	بدم	*I give*

2.3 Let's Talk
[02sect3]

As in English, there are four types of demonstrative adjectives in Farsi. These are **ān** آن (*that*), **in** این (*this*), **ānhā** آنها (*those*), and **inhā** اینها (*these*). Also, as we learned in the last section, Farsi speakers often colloquially use the term **oon** اون instead of **ān** آن (*that*). For example, in the Conversation section, Daniel said,
Nasrin az oon tāxi bepors. نسرین از اون تاکسی بپرس (*Nasrin, ask that taxi*).

Now let's build some Farsi phrases, using demonstrative pronouns with the words you have learned so far. Read and repeat to yourself the following sentences. The shaded letters show the demonstrative pronouns.

a. in āghā این آقا
    this man

b. ān hotel آن هتل
    that hotel

c. in khānoom این خانوم
    this woman

d. ānhā khaliānd آنها خالیند
    those are empty

e. Inhā misheh si hezar tomān. اینها میشه سی هزار تومان
    These will be thirty thousand tomans.

f. In daro bāz kon. این در رو باز کن.
    Open this door.

Some Farsi pleasantries are very difficult to translate into English. They have to be learned as they are. Let us study some of them to see what they mean and how they can be used in different circumstances.

i. **taghdim kardan** تقدیم کردن
    This expression can have a wide range of meanings, such as to offer, present, pay, and bring. It usually means, "I will deliver or give something to you with pleasure." For instance, Nasrin said to the taxi driver, **Che ghadr** taghdim konam? چه قدر تقدیم کنم؟ *How much can I offer you?*

ii. **ghābel nadāshtan** قابل نداشتن
    This expression is similar to the English phrase *Don't mention it*. You would use it in places where you do not want to give someone a bad feeling because you helped them, offered to do them a favor, or gave them money or a gift. For instance, in the conversation, when Nasrin wants to pay for the ride, the taxi driver says, **Befarmāeed,** ghābel nadāreh. بفرمایید، قابل نداره. *Please, it is not worth mentioning.*

Did you notice that in the conversation, both Daniel and the taxi driver used the French word **merci** مرسی to say *thank you*? In fact there are many French loanwords which have found their way into modern Farsi. These words are usually used by middle and upper-class people in the capital Tehran or big urban areas.

2.4 The Letters *Jim*, *Che*, *Heh*, and *Khe*

[02sect4]

Now, we will learn four new letters. These letters are very similar in form. In fact, their only difference is whether they have dots, and the placement of these dots if they have them.

■ The letter jim ج

The letter **jim** ج is pronounced like the "j" in the English word "jam." The following table shows the different forms of the letter **jim** ج. Learn the letter, and practice the pronunciation, and remember the meaning of each word.

Position	Form	As in	Pronounced	Meaning
Initial	جـ	جـا	**jā**	*place*
Medial	ـجـ	کجا	**ko**jā	*where*
Final	ـج	لج	**la**j	*grudge*
Independent	ج	تاج	**tā**j	*crown*

■ The letter che چ

The letter **che** چ is pronounced like the "ch" in "China." The following table shows the different forms of the letter **che** چ . Learn the letter, practice the pronunciation, and remember the meaning of each word.

Position	Form	As in	Pronounced	Meaning
Initial	ﭼ	چه	che	*what*
Medial	ﭼ	کچل	kachal	*bald*
Final	ﭻ	مچ	moch	*wrist*
Independent	چ	پارچ	pārch	*jar*

■ The letter heh ح

The letter **heh** ح is pronounced like the "h" in the English word "home." Pay attention that this letter does not have any dots, either above or under it. The following table shows the different forms of the letter **heh** ح . Learn the letter, practice the pronunciation, and remember the meaning of each word.

Position	Form	As in	Pronounced	Meaning
Initial	ﺣ	حالا	hālā	*now*
Medial	ﺤ	سحر	sahar	*dawn*
Final	ﺢ	صبح	sobh	*morning*
Independent	ح	شرح	sharh	*description*

■ The letter khe خ

The letter **khe** خ does not have a counterpart in the English alphabet, and is often difficult for English speakers to pronounce. The sound is similar to the sound of the letter "j" in the Spanish name "Juan." For transliteration purposes, we have shown this letter as "kh." Listen to the recordings and try to imitate the sound of the letter **khe** خ as well as you can. The following table shows the different forms of the letter **khe** خ. Learn the letter, practice the pronunciation, and remember the meaning of each word.

Position	Form	As in	Pronounced	Meaning
Initial	خـ	خدا	khodā	God
Medial	ـخـ	سخت	sakht	hard
Final	ـخ	میخ	mikh	nail
Independent	خ	شاخ	shākh	horn

Now practice writing the letter **heh** ح first, and then add dots to convert **heh** ح into **jim** ج, **che** چ, and **khe** خ.

2.5 Let's Write

In this chapter, we learned four new letters which looked very similar in form. Now let's combine these letters with other letters you learned in the previous chapter to create words in Farsi. The following table consists of three columns. From right to left (in the Farsi way), the first column shows the letters we want to combine in their independent forms. The second column shows what form each letter should have based on its placement in the word. Finally, the third column indicates how the actual Farsi word looks when these letters are connected. Note that the following words may not have any particular meanings. We just want to learn how to write Farsi letters and words.

Words	Letters in proper position	Letters in independent form
حس	حـ ـس	ح س
مچ	مـ ـچ	م چ
ماچ	مـ ـا چ	م ا چ
مجسم	مـ ـجـ ـسـ ـم	م س ج م
لجام	لـ ـجـ ـا م	ل ج ا م
چال	چـ ـا ل	چ ا ل

Now, fill in the last column of the following table with the letters provided.

Words	Letters in proper position	Letters in independent form
a.	ل ج خ	ل ج خ
b.	ج ا ل ج ل	ج ا ج ل
c.	ل ا چ	ل ا چ
d.	ل ح م	ل ح م
e.	م ح ل	م ح ل

From now on, we will replace some of the important words with their actual Farsi words within the English texts. The idea is to encourage you, one step at a time, to build up your reading ability in Farsi. First you will see an English word in italics. That word is followed by parentheses. Inside the parentheses, first you see a transliteration of that word in Farsi and then the same word using Farsi script. Remember how that word is pronounced and written. The next instances of that word in the same text will only show the Farsi script (without any transliteration or English meaning).

2.6 Cultural Insight

Har māchini mitavānad yek tāxi bāshad.
هر ماشینی می‌تواند یک تاکسی باشد.
Every car can be a taxi.

In Iran, especially in the capital *Tehran* (**Tehrān** تهران), many private cars serve the function of taxis. Passengers hold up their hands in the main streets to show that they need a ride. Official taxis as well as private cars stop to amass *passengers* (plural **mosāferān** مسافران, singular **mosāfer** مسافر), sometimes as many as four to a car. Most cars only go in *direct* (**mostaghim** مستقیم) routes or between major landmarks in the cities, and as such shared rides become more manageable. However, مسافران very often need to take two or three rides in order to get to their destinations.

The *fare* (**kerāyeh** کرایه) can be relatively *cheap* (**arzān** ارزان) for these rides, and private drivers use the money to supplement their income while driving in the city. The official currency of Iran is called *rial* (**Riāl** ریال). However, as was mentioned in the Conversation, people frequently use the word *toman* (**Tomān** تومان) instead of ریال. Each تومان is equal to 10 ریال. There are other forms of taxis that are more similar to American taxis, which are called **ājānce** (from the French word **agence** which means **agency** in English, آژانس), and there are *phone taxis* (**tāxi telephoni** تاکسی تلفنی) which are called in advance to pick up passengers.

 2.7 Vocabulary
[02sect7]

In this section, read the words in Farsi and memorize their meaning. Then play back the audio and check your pronunciation. You can use this section as a reference if you have a question about the meaning of the words in the Conversation section.

Transliteration	Farsi	Meaning
bepors	بپرس	*ask*
āghā	آقا	*Mr./Sir*
khāli	خالی	*empty/available*
khanoom	خانم	*Mrs./Ma'am*
biāeed bālā	بیایید بالا	*come up/get on*
dar	در	*door*
baz kon	باز کن	*open*
dastam bandeh.	دستم بنده	*My hands are full*
hotel	هتل	*hotel*
bebarid	ببرید	*take* (plural)
merci	مرسی	*Thank you*
piādeh mishim	پیاده میشیم	*we get off*

Transliteration	Farsi	Meaning
che ghadr	چقدر	*how much*
taghdim konam	تقدیم کنم	*I offer*
befarmāeed	بفرمایید	*please/sit down/enter/say*
ghābel nadāreh	قابل نداره	*It is not worth mentioning*
khāhesh mikonam	خواهش می‌کنم	*please/I ask/you are welcome*
si	سی	*thirty*
hezār	هزار	*thousand*
misheh	میشه	*it is*
pool	پول	*money*
dāri	داری	*you have*
anām bedam?	انعام بدم؟	*Should I tip?*
dost dāri	دوست داری	*you like*
khosh begozarad	خوش بگذرد	*Have fun/Have a nice stay*
khodāhafez	خداحافظ	*Goodbye*

2.8 Grammar Point: Personal Pronouns

In the Conversation section, participants used different pronouns to address other people. The following table denotes subject personal pronouns in Farsi.

Singular pronouns		Plural pronouns	
man (I)	من	**mā** (we)	ما
to (you)	تو	**shomā** (you all)	شما
oo (he, she, it)	او	**ānhā** (they)	انها

The plural second person pronoun **shomā** شما (you all) is frequently used instead of the singular second person pronoun **to** تو (you) to show respect. In the Conversation section, Daniel also used شما when he said to the taxi driver, **Khedmate** shomā خدمت شما (Here you are). Then, when the taxi driver addressed the Paradise family, he said, Shomā **kojā mirid** میرید کجا شما (Where are you going?). In this case, the use of شما is not just out of respect, but because the driver is addressing more than one person.

You should also note that there is no gender marking in Farsi. Therefore, the third person singular for a female, a male, or a subject pronoun is always **oo** او. Occasionally, Farsi speakers use the demonstrative adjective **ān** آن (that) instead of او to refer to an object.

2.9 Zarbol masal (*Proverb*) of the Day

[02sect9]

Tārof āmad nayāmad dāreh. تعارف آمد نیامد داره.
The "tārof" may or may not come. (Tārof may be accepted or refused.)

There is a complex cultural practice in Iran called **tārof** تعارف, which includes a host of pleasantries, acts of politeness, and formalities toward others. For instance, when two or more people are passing through a door, they offer to the other person the chance to enter first by saying **Avval shomā** اول شما (*You first*) or **Shomā befarmāeed** شما بفرمایید (*Please, you enter*). Furthermore, it is considered very disrespectful to accept food, drink, money, or help from others upon first offer. Customarily, one has to refrain from accepting an offer until it is extended at least twice, and sometimes even several times.

In the Conversation section, when Daniel offered to pay for the cab ride, the taxi driver responded by saying **Befarmāeed ghābele shomāro nadāreh** بفرمایید، قابل شمارو نداره *(Please, it is not worth mentioning)*. The taxi driver's response is an act of **tārof** تعارف. Almost all taxi drivers will refuse to accept money upon first offer, and all passengers know that they have to insist in order to pay for the ride. However, in offering and refusing, sometimes one might, for example, offer politely to give his lunch to another person, expecting this offer to be refused. However, this polite تعارف gesture may be mistaken for a genuine offer and eventually accepted, leaving the person who offered the food without lunch. People use the expression **Tārof āmad nayāmad dāreh** تعارف آمد نیامد دارد to caution others not to insist *too* much about something they do not really mean to offer, but are just trying to be polite about.

2.10 Exercises

1. Find and write down the personal pronouns in the Conversation section, using Farsi script.

    _____

2. What are the various forms of the pronoun "you" in Farsi, and what are their differences?

    _____

3. Read the following words out loud and check your pronunciation against the Conversation recording.

a. **Khānoom**
b. **Khāli**
c. **Khāhesh mikonam**
d. **Khedmat**
e. **Khosh begozarad**
f. **Khodā hāfez**

4. You already know all the letters used to construct the following combinations. Try to guess how they should be pronounced by writing down their transliterations.

Example : سم
Answer : sam

a. _____ حال

b. _____ جسم

c. _____ جام

d. _____ خم

e. _____ مال

f. _____ سال

g. _____ سمج

h. _____ خام

i. _____ مخ

j. _____ چال

Responses to writing practice in section 2.5:

Words

a. خجل

b. لجاج

c. چال

d. محل

e. لحم

Mokālemeh telefoni
مکالمه تلفنی
Phone Calls

In this chapter, we will learn more new letters and learn about short and long vowels in Farsi. In the Grammar section, we will learn how to form *wh*-questions in Farsi. And, we will discuss expressions and customs regarding phone conversations in Iranian culture.

3.1 Conversation
[03dia]

Barnāmehrizie shām
برنامه ریزی شام
Arranging a dinner party

Listen to the conversation first. Then replay the audio, this time reading along with the text below. In this chapter, Nasrin calls her mom from her hotel room to ask to have dinner at her place. Mrs. Rahmati suggests to invite her other daughter, Manijeh, and her kids to the dinner party.

NASRIN:	**Māmān joon* salām. Nasrinam*.** *Hello, dear Mommy. It's Nasrin.*	مامان جون* سلام. نسرینم*.
MRS. RAHMATI:	**Salām dokhtaram. Residid hotel?** *Hello my daughter. Did you arrive at the hotel?*	سلام دخترم. رسیدید هتل؟
NASRIN:	**Āreh. Hamin alān residim.** *Yes, we just got there.*	آره. همین الان رسیدیم.
MRS. RAHMATI:	**Bekhodā nabāyad miraftid hotel.** *I swear, you shouldn't have gone to a hotel.*	بخدا نباید می‌رفتید هتل.
NASRIN:	**Injoori hamamoon* rāhat-tarim*.** *Everyone's more comfortable this way.*	اینجوری هممون* راحتتریم*.
MRS. RAHMATI:	**Barnāmatoon* barāye fardā chieh*?** *What's your plan for tomorrow?*	برنامه تون* برای فردا چیه*؟
NASRIN:	**Mikhāhim barāye shām mozāhemetoon* beshim*.** *We want to trouble you for dinner.*	می خواهیم برای شام مزاحمتون* بشیم*.

MRS. RAHMATI:	Ghadametoon* rooyeh cheshm.	قدمتون* روی چشم.
	You're most welcome. (Literally: "Your steps on my eyes.")	
MRS. RAHMATI:	Mikhāhee māchin bābāto* dāshteh bāshee?	میخواهی ماشین باباتو* داشته باشی؟
	Do you want to use your dad's car?	
NASRIN:	Na, mozāheme kār o zendegitoon* nemishim*.	نه، مزاحم کار و زندگیتون* نمیشیم*.
	No, we don't [want to] become burden to your life and work.	
MRS. RAHMATI:	Behar hāl bābāt* ke digeh* kār nemikoneh*.	بهر حال بابات* که دیگه* کار نمیکنه*.
	In any case, your dad is no longer working.	
NASRIN:	Na yek ājānce migirim.	نه یک آژانس می گیریم.
	No, we will get a taxi.	
Mrs. Rahmati:	Mikhāi* Manijeh inhā-ro* ham davat konam?	میخوای* منیژه اینها رو* هم دعوت کنم؟
	Do you want me to invite Manijeh and her family?	
NASRIN:	Ākheh* digeh* kheili sakhtetoon* misheh*.	آخه* دیگه* خیلی سختتون* میشه*.
	But you are going to put yourself to too much trouble.	
MRS. RAHMATI:	Na tāzeh Manizheh ham komakam mikoneh*.	نه تازه منیژه هم کمکم میکنه*.
	No, Manizheh can help me.	
NASRIN:	To rā bekhodā khodet ro* be zahmat nandāz*.	تو را بخدا خودت رو* به زحمت ننداز*.
	In God's name, do not put yourself to the trouble.	
MRS. RAHMATI:	Na negarān nabāsh. Faghat zood biāeed.	نه نگران نباش. فقط زود بیایید.
	No, don't worry. Just arrive early.	
NASRIN:	Bāsheh*. Khodāfez*.	باشه*. خدافظ*.
	Ok. Bye.	
MRS. RAHMATI:	Khodāfez* tā fardā.	خدافظ* تا فردا.
	Bye. See you tomorrow.	

3.2 Formal vs. Colloquial: Words from the Conversation

The colloquial forms of the words (محاوره ای **mohāverei**) in the Conversation have been marked with an asterisk (*). While reading the Conversation, consider the context in which a colloquial word has been used. Then, study the formal forms (رسمی **rasmi**) to become familiar with the way you would address a person formally, or would find that word in a Farsi book or a newspaper.

Formal	رسمی	Colloquial*	محاوره ای *	Meaning
māmān jān	مامان جان	māmān joon	مامان جون	*dear Mom*
Nasrin hastam	نسرین هستم	Nasrinam	نسرینم	*I am Nasrin*
hame-emān	همه مان	hamamoon	هممون	*all of us*
rāhat-tar hastim	راحتتر هستیم	rāhat-tarim	راحتتریم	*We are more comfortable*
barnāme-etān	برنامه تان	barnāmatoon	برنامه تون	*your plan*
cheh ast?	چه است؟	chieh?	چیه؟	*What is it?*
mozāhem-etān	مزاحم تان	mozāhemetoon	مزاحمتون	*your trouble*
beshavim	بشویم	beshim	بشیم	*we become*
ghadame-tān	قدمتان	ghadametoon	قدمتون	*your steps*
bābāyat	بابایت	bābāt	بابات	*your father's*
bābāye torā	بابای تو را	bābāto	باباتو	your father's + **ra** (a proposition)
zendegi-etān	زندگی تان	zendegitoon	زندگیتون	*your life*
nemishavim	نمی‌شویم	nemishim	نمیشیم	*we won't be*
digar	دیگر	digeh	دیگه	*no longer*
kār nemikonad	کار نمی کند	kār nemikoneh	کارنمیکنه	*does not work*
mikhāhi	می‌خواهی	mikhāi	میخوای	*do you want*

Formal	رسمی	Colloquial*	محاوره ای*	Meaning
rā	را	ro	رو	(a preposition)
sakhte-etan	سخت تان	sakhtetoon	سختتون	*your hardship*
mishavad	می‌شود	misheh	میشه	*it becomes*
komak mikonad	کمکم می‌کند	komak mikoneh	کمکم میکنه	*he/she/it helps me*
zahmat nayandāz	زحمت نینداز	zahmat nandāz	زحمت ننداز	*Don't trouble yourself*
bāshad	باشد	bāsheh	باشه	*Let it be*
khodāhafez	خداحافظ	khodāfez	خدافظ	*bye*

3.3 Let's Talk

[03sect3]

From the Conversation, you might have noticed that the word **na** نه in Farsi means *no* in English. Similarly, in order to make a verb negative in Farsi, you just need to add the letter "n" ن to its beginning. For instance, Nasrin told Mrs. Rahmati, **Na, mozāheme kār o zendegitoon ne**mishim نمیشیم نه، مزاحم کار و زندگیتون (*No, we don't [want to] become burden to your life and work*). First, there is the word **na**, and then the verb **nemishim** at the end of the sentence, which is constructed from **ne** and **mishim**. As you just learned in the above table, **mishim** is a colloquial way of saying **misahvim** (*we will be or we will become*). The **ne** makes this verb negative: **ne**mishim or **ne**mishavim (*we won't be or we won't become*).

Conversely, you can affirm an action or statement either by saying **āreh** آره or **baleh** بله (*yes*). For instance, Mrs. Rahmati asked her daughter, **Salām dokhtaram. Residid hotel?** سلام دخترم. رسیدید هتل؟ (*Hello my daughter. Did you arrive at the hotel?*). And Nasrin affirmed her mother's question by saying,

Āreh. Hamin alān residim آره همین الان رسیدیم (*Yes, we just got there*).

Baleh بله is a more polite way of saying *yes*. **Āreh** آره is reserved for informal conversations and among close relatives.

Now let's practice using **āreh**, **baleh**, and **na** with the words we have learned so far. Read and practice the following sentences.

a.   **Residid be hotel?** ‏رسیدید به هتل؟‏
Did you get to the hotel?

   Na, hanooz naresidim. ‏نه، هنوز نرسیدیم.‏
No, we have not arrived yet.

b.   **Mikhāhid fardā bā ham shām bekhorim?** ‏می‌خواهید فردا باهم شام بخوریم؟‏
Do you want us to have dinner together tomorrow?

   Baleh, kheili doost dāram. ‏بله، خیلی دوست دارم.‏
Yes, I would like it very much.

c.   **Mikhāi barāt ye tāxi begiram?** ‏میخوای برات یه تاکسی بگیرم؟‏
Do you want me to get a taxi for you?

   Āreh, barām ye tāxi begir. ‏آره، برام یه تاکسی بگیر.‏
Yes, please get a taxi for me.

[03sect4]

3.4 Short and Long Vowels, and the Letters *Dāl* and *Zāl*

Farsi consists of six vowels. Three of these are considered long vowels, and three are considered short vowels. In Farsi, long vowels are written. However, short vowels are not written, but have to be guessed. In Chapter 1, we discussed one of the long vowels, ‏آ‏ ("ā"). The other two long vowels are ‏ی‏ and ‏و‏.

■ The long vowel ie ی

The vowel **ie** ی is pronounced like the "ee" in the English word "been." In the following table, you will learn different forms of the letter ی. Read and reexamine how this letter changes form depending on its place in a word. Note that in its initial and medial forms, this letter has two dots, but in the final and independent forms, it does not have any dots and it also changes shape.

Position	Form	As in	Pronounced	Meaning
Initial	یـ	یاس	yās	*jasmine*
Medial	ـیـ	بیا	biā	*come*
Final	ـی	سی	si	*thirty*
Independent	ی	پری	pari	*fairy*

■ The long vowel u و

The vowel **u** و is pronounced like the "oo" in the English word "pool." Like the vowel **a** ا, the vowel **u** و only has a final and an independent form. Study the following table to see how these two forms are used in words.

Position	Form	As in	Pronounced	Meaning
Final	ـو	جون	joon	*dear/life*
Independent	و	زود	zood	*early/quick*

Now practice writing the different forms of the long vowels **u** و and **ie** ی.

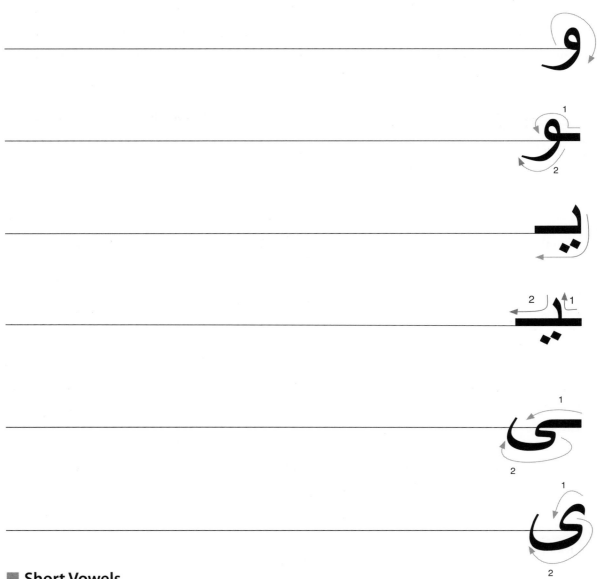

■ Short Vowels

By now, you might have suspected that many Farsi words have hidden vowels, vowels which are pronounced but not written. For instance, the word **dar** در (*door*) has a short, unwritten vowel. This short vowel sounds like the "a" in the English word "cat," and is called **fat-heh**. فتحه. Another short vowel, called **kasreh** کسره, sounds like the "e" in the English word "bed." The last short vowel is called **zammeh** ضَمّه, and sounds like the "o" in the English word "home."

For example, the Farsi word **del** دل (*heart*) is written with only two consonants, "d" د and "l" ل. However, these two letters are connected with a short and unwritten **kasreh** کسره, and so the word is pronounced **del** دل. And, in the word **moch** مچ (*wrist*), there is an unwritten "o" which connects the "m" م to the "ch" چ.

Occasionally, these short vowels are written in children's books and dictionaries as diacritics above and under the letters to help novice readers learn the correct pronunciation of the words. In the beginning, it may be somewhat difficult to read Farsi words without the use of these diacritics. However, eventually it will be much easier to learn the pronunciation of the whole word rather than trying to spell out each individual letter while trying to figure out their corresponding short vowels. Hence, in this book we do not use these diacritics.

In the Conversation section, you might have noticed that sometimes we write the long vowel **u** و, but we do not pronounce it. For example, Nasrin said, **Mikhāhim barāye shām mozāhemetoon beshim** می‌خواهیم برای شام مزاحمتون بشیم (*We want to trouble you for dinner*). Look closely at the word **mikhāhim**. As you can see, there is a **u** و in می‌خواهیم, but the word is pronounced as though the **u** does not exist. You will often see this when the **u** و is followed by the long vowel **ā** ا, such as in the words **khāb** خواب (*sleep*), **khāndan** خواندن (*to read*), **khāstan** خواستن (*to want*), and **khāhar** خواهر (*sister*).

■ The letter dāl د

The letter **dāl** د is pronounced like the "d" in the English word "dog," and has only two forms, final and independent. Study the following table to see how these two forms are written in Farsi words.

Position	Form	As in	Pronounced	Meaning
Final	ـد	بد	ba**d**	*bad*
Independent	د	فردا	far**d**ā	*tomorrow*

Note that the "a" in the word "**bad**" is a short vowel, and is unwritten in Farsi. There are, however, two forms of "a" in the word "**fardā**." The first "a" is a short vowel and is unwritten, while the second "a" is a long vowel and written as ا.

Although there are some common words and derivatives between English and Farsi, the similarity of the sound and meaning of the word "bad" in both languages in the above example appears to be just a linguistic coincidence.

■ The letter zāl ذ

The letter **zāl** ذ is pronounced like the "z" in the English word "zoo," and has only two forms. There are three other Farsi letters that sound exactly like **zāl** (ض, ز, and ظ), which we will be studying in future chapters. Study the following table to see how these two forms of the letter **zāl** ذ are written in Farsi words.

Position	Form	As in	Pronounced	Meaning
Final	ذ	بذر	ba**z**r	*seed*
Independent	ذ	ذهن	**z**ehn	*mind*

Now practice writing the letter **dāl**, and then place dots over the letters to convert **dāl** into **zāl**.

3.5 Let's Write

Now let's combine the letters we have learned in this chapter with the letters from previous chapters to create new words. In the following table, from right to left, the first column shows the letters we want to combine, in their independent forms. The second column shows what form each letter should have based on its placement in the word. You just have to fill in the last column by attaching them together. An example has been provided in the first row.

Words	Letters in proper position	Letters in independent form
a. حد	حـد	ح د
b.	خـدا	خ ا د
c.	وادى	و ا د ى
d.	دوا	د و ا
e.	حـاوى	ح ا و ى
f.	ذلـيـل	ذ ل ى ل
g.	مـلـس	م ل س
h.	سـيـل	س ى ل
i.	مـدال	م د ا ل
j.	مـخـمـل	م خ م ل
k.	سـيـمـا	س ى م ا

3.6 Cultural Insight: Iranian Phone Calls

Closely related to the concept of **tārof** تعارف, which was discussed in the previous chapter, greetings and farewells in Farsi are very lengthy and formal. For instance, **friends** (plural **doostān** دوستان, singular **doost** دوست) and family members start a phone conversation by not only asking about one's health, **Hālet khoobeh?** حالت خوبه؟ (*How are you?*), but also about the health of close members of each other's family, such as parents, siblings, and children.

A typical phone conversation between two related people usually includes questions such as, **Hāle māmān va bābā khoobeh?** حال مامان و بابا خوبه؟ (*Are your mom and dad ok?*), **Bachehā chetorand?** بچّه ها چطورند؟ (*How are the kids?*), and questions about the other party's siblings, for example, **Az Manijeh joon che khabar?** از منیژه جون چه خبر؟ (*Any news about dear Manijeh?*). It is only then that one can start delivering the real intended message for the phone call, for example, **Mikhāstam doshanbeh barāye shām davatetoon konam.** می‌خواستم دوشنبه برای شام دعوتتون کنم. (*I wanted to invite you for dinner on Monday*).

A phone conversation is similarly terminated by saluting the extended members of the one's family. For instance, one would close a phone conversation by saying, **Be māmāno bābā salām beresonid.** به مامان و بابا سلام برسونید. (*Send my greetings to your mom and dad*), **Bacheh hāro az jānebe man beboosid.** بچه هارو از جانب من ببوسید. (*Kiss your children on my behalf*), and **Torā bekhodā be Manijeh joon begid ye yādi az mā bekoneh** ترا بخدا به منیژه جون بگید یه یادی از ما بکنه. (*In God's name, please tell dear Manijeh to remember us some time*).

3.7 Vocabulary
[03sect7]

In this section, read the words in Farsi and memorize their meaning. Then play back the audio and check your pronunciation. You can use this section as a reference if you have a question about the meaning of the words in the Conversation section.

Transliteration	Farsi	Meaning
dokhtar	دختر	*daughter*
residid	رسیدید	*you arrived (pl.)*
alān	الان	*now*
bāyad	باید	*must*
miraftid	می‌رفتید	*you went*
rāhat	راحت	*easy/convenient*
barnāmeh	برنامه	*plan/agenda*
mikhāhim	می‌خواهیم	*we want*
shām	شام	*dinner*
māchin	ماشین	*car*
beharhāl	بهرحال	*any way*
digeh	دیگه	*next/other/another/any*
zahmat	زحمت	*trouble*
davat konam	دعوت کنم	*I invite*
ākheh	آخه	*but*
kheili	خیلی	*very/a lot*
sakht	سخت	*difficult*

Transliteration	Farsi	Meaning
komak	کمک	*help*
negarān	نگران	*worry*
faghat	فقط	*only*
zood	زود	*early/soon/quick*

3.8 Grammar Point: *When, Where, What, Why*, and *How*

Wh-question words are commonly used in all languages. The following table shows the *wh*-question words in English, followed by their counterparts in Farsi. While studying this table, go back and look in this and previous chapters to find any use of these words. Note that both *who* and *when* are written in Farsi as کی, but are pronounced differently.

Transliteration	Farsi	English
ki	کی	*who*
key	کی	*when*
kojā	کجا	*where*
cheh/chi	چه\چی	*what*
cherā	چرا	*why*
chegooneh/che joori	چگونه\چه جوری	*how*

3.9 Expression of the Day

[03sect9]

Ghadametoon royeh cheshm قدمتون روی چشم
Your steps on my eyes

The **chashm** چشم (*eye*) in Iranian culture is considered one of the most sensitive parts of the *body* (**badan** بدن), and the word **chashm** چشم is often used as an expression of showing sensitivity toward others. For instance, children often say **chashm** چشم instead of **baleh** بله (*yes*) when responding positively to an adult's command. The word **chashm** چشم here means, "I accept your request without challenge."

Similarly, Farsi speakers may say **Ghadametoon royeh cheshm** قدمتون روی چشم (*Your steps on my eyes*) to welcome someone with utmost *respect* (**ehterām** احترام). In the Conversation section, Nasrin informed her mother that she wanted to come to her home for dinner, **Mikhāhim baraye shām mozāhemetoon beshim** می‌خواهیم برای شام مزاحمتون بشیم (*We want to trouble you for dinner*). Mrs. Rahmati welcomed her daughter's request by stating, **Ghadametoon royeh cheshm** قدمتون روی چشم. By this expression, Mrs. Rahmati intends to say that she welcomes her daughter's family to her home with great pleasure.

3.10 Exercises

1. The following words have been taken from the Conversation of this chapter. They all use short vowels, which are pronounced but not written. Try to guess the correct pronunciation of these words by writing down their English transliterations.

    Example: چشم
    Answer: chashm

    a. _____ دخترم

    b. _____ هم

    c. _____ یک

    d. _____ سر

    e. _____ هتل

2. The following words have been taken from the Conversation of this chapter. They all use long vowels. Find the long vowel, guess its sound, and say the whole word in Farsi.

a. _____ همین

b. _____ جون

c. _____ تا

d. _____ کار

e. _____ چیه

3. The following are Farsi transliterations. Rewrite these words using Farsi letters.

Example: **dād** داد

a. **zam** _____

b. **jad** _____

c. **khodā** _____

d. **zāl** _____

4. Read these Farsi phrases with *wh*-question words and guess their meanings.

a. _____ کی رسیدید؟

b. _____ کجا می‌رفتید؟

c. _____ چه جوری دارند می‌آیند؟

d. _____ چرا دوستش داری؟

Responses to writing practice in section 3.5:

Words

a. حد

b. خدا

c. وادی

d. دوا

e. حاوی

f. ذلیل

g. ملس

h. سیل

i. مدال

j. مخمل

k. سیما

Māh va fasl
ماه و فصل
Months and Seasons

In this chapter, we will learn more Farsi letters and also become familiar with the names of the days, months (such as Farvardin, Ordibehesht, and Khordad that correspond to March, April, and May, respectively), and seasons in Farsi. Related to this topic, we will talk about the importance of spring in Iranian culture, and discuss why the Iranian New Year starts in spring.

4.1 Conversation

[04dia]

Key va kojā
کی و کجا
When and where

Daniel, Nasrin, and Sara are having breakfast in their hotel while discussing plans for their stay in Iran. They talk about visiting a major city in the south of Iran called Shiraz and a hike to a mountain top called Tochal. Listen to the Conversation first, and then replay the audio, this time reading along with the text below.

SARA:	**Emrooz mikhām* bāzār rā bebinām.** *Today, I want to see the bazaar.*	.امروز میخوام* بازار را ببینم
DANIEL:	**Shāyad doshanbeh behtar bāsheh*.** *Maybe Monday would be better.*	.*شاید دوشنبه بهتر باشه
NASRIN:	**Avval bāyad fāmil ro* bebinim.** *First, we have to see the family.*	.اوّل باید فامیل رو* ببینیم
DANIEL:	**Chand rooz Tehrān mimoonim*?** *How many days are we staying in Tehran?*	چند روز تهران میمونیم*؟
NASRIN:	**Fekr konam* yek hafteh khoobe*.** *I think one week is good.*	.*فکرکنم* یک هفته خوبه
NASRIN:	**Chon tābestāne* avval berim* shomāl.** *Since it is summer, first we should go to shomal (the Caspian Sea region).*	.چون تابستانه*، اوّل بریم* شمال

SARA:	**Bachehāye khāle Manijeh ham miānd*?**	بچّه های خاله منیژه هم میاند*؟
	Will Aunt Manijeh's kids also come?	
NASRIN:	**Emshab az māmānesh miporsim.**	امشب از مامانش می پرسیم.
	Tonight, we'll ask her mom.	
DANIEL:	**Che fasli barāye didane esfahān khobe*?**	چه فصلی برای دیدن اصفهان خوبه*؟
	What season is best to go to Esfahan?	
NASRIN:	**Fekr mikonam bahār behtar bāsheh*.**	فکر می‌کنم بهار بهتر باشه*.
	I think spring is better.	
DANIEL:	**Mesle Farvardin yā Ordibehesht?**	مثل فروردین یا اردیبهشت؟
	For instance, Farvardin or Ordibehesht?	
NASRIN:	**Āreh, vali Khordād ham khoobe*.**	آره، ولی خرداد هم خوبه*.
	Yes, but Khordad is also good.	
SARA:	**Māmān to gofti ke mitoonim* berim* kooh.**	مامان تو گفتی که میتونیم* بریم* کوه.
	Mom, you said we could go to the mountains [to hike].	
NASRIN:	**Āreh, shāyad jomeh berim* Tochāl.**	آره، شاید جمعه بریم* توچال.
	Yes, maybe we will go to Tochal on Friday.	
DANIEL:	**Shirāz ra ham kheili doost dāram bebinam.**	شیراز را هم خیلی دوست دارم ببینم.
	I really want to see Shiraz as well.	
NASRIN:	**Bad az Esfahān, be Shirāz mirim*.**	بعد از اصفهان، به شیراز میریم*.
	After Esfahan, we will go to Shiraz.	
DANIEL:	**Sārā, agar sobhānat* tamām shod, berim*.**	سارا، اگر صبحانت* تمام شد، بریم*.
	Sara, if you are done with breakfast, let's go.	
SARA:	**Āreh bābā. berim* shahr rā bebinim.**	آره بابا، بریم* شهر را ببینیم.
	Yes Daddy. Let's go and see the city.	

[04sect2]

4.2 Formal vs. Colloquial: Words from the Conversation

The colloquial forms of the words (محاوره ای **mohāverei**) in the Conversation have been marked with an asterisk (*). While reading the conversation, consider the context in which a colloquial word has been used. Then, study the formal forms (رسمی **rasmi**) to become familiar with the way you would address a person formally, or would find that word in a Farsi book or a newspaper.

Formal	رسمی	Colloquial*	محاوره ای*	Meaning
mikhāham	می‌خواهم	mikhām	میخوام	*I want*
bāshad	باشد	bāsheh	باشه	*let it be*
rā	را	ro	رو	*of/from*
mimānim	می‌مانیم	mimoonim	میمونیم	*we stay*
fekr mikonam	فکر می‌کنم	fekr konam	فکرکنم	*I think*
khoob ast	خوب است	khoobeh	خوبه	*is good*
tābestān ast	تابستان است	tābestāneh	تابستانه	*is summer*
beravim	برویم	berim	بریم	*let's go*
miāyand	می‌آیند	miānd	میاند	*they come*
mitavānim	می‌توانیم	mitoonim	میتونیم	*we can*
miravim	می‌رویم	mirim	میریم	*we go*
sobhāneh-at	صبحانه ات	sobhānat	صبحانت	*your breakfast*

 **4.3 Let's Talk**

[04sect3]

In Farsi, you show intention with the verb **khāstan** خواستن (*to want*). The following table shows the conjugation of the verb **khāstan** خواستن.

Transliteration	Farsi	Meaning
mikhāham	می خواهم	*I want*
mikhāhi	می خواهی	*you want*
mikhāhad	می خواهد	*she/he/it wants*
mikhāhim	می خواهیم	*we want*
mikhāhid	می خواهید	*you want (pl.)*
mikhāhand	می خواهند	*they want*

In the previous section, we saw that the colloquial form of **mikhāham** is **mikhām**. For example, in the beginning of the Conversation, Sara says, **Emrooz** mikhām **bāzār rā bebinām** امروز میخوام بازار را ببینم (*Today, I want to see the bazaar*).

Now, let us practice this new verb. Read and repeat to yourself the following sentences.

a. Mikhāham **beram hotel homā.**
   می خواهم برم هتل هما.
   I want to go to Hotel Homa.

b. Mikhāhi **berim shomāl?**
   می خواهی بریم شمال؟
   Do you want us to go to the north?

c. Mikhād **shahr ro bebineh.**
   میخواد شهر رو ببینه.
   He/she wants to see the city.

d. Mikhāhim **bāzār berim.**
   می خواهیم بازار بریم.
   We want to go to the bazaar.

e.   Mikhāhand **tanhā bāshand.**

می خواهند تنها باشند.

They want to be alone.

f.   Mikhāhid **tāxi begirim?**

می خواهید تاکسی بگیریم؟

Do you (pl.) want us to take a taxi?

g.   Man va doostam mikhāhim **Shirāz berim.**

من و دوستام می خواهیم شیراز بریم.

My friend and I want to go to Shiraz.

h.   Kojā mikhāhi **berim?**

کجا می خواهی بریم؟

Where do you want us to go?

As you may have noticed from the previous examples, for the most part questions in Farsi have the same grammatical structure as statements, but use a rising intonation to turn a statement into a question. While listening to the conversations on the audio, pay close attention to the rising tone in interrogative sentences. Since there is no general rule regarding the part of speech that takes this rising tone, you need to get a feeling for it by listening continuously to a native speaker talk in Farsi. The accompanying audio provides some examples for you.

 4.4 The Letters *Re*, *Zeh*, *Zheh*, *Kāf*, and *Gāf*
[04sect4]

We will now learn more Farsi letters, some of which were frequently used in the Conversation section. These letters can be divided into two categories. The letters **re** ر, **ze** ز, and **zhe** ژ have similar forms, and only differ in the number (or its absence) of dots placed above them. The letters **kāf** ک and **gāf** گ also have similar forms, but the letter **gāf** گ has a strike above its top line.

■ The letter re ر

The letter **re** ر is pronounced like the "r" in the English word "rich," and has only two forms, final and independent. The following table shows the different forms of the letter **re** ر as it is used in words. Learn the letter, practice the pronunciation, and remember the meaning of each word.

Position	Form	As in	Pronounced	Meaning
Final	ـر	مرد	ma**r**d	*man*
Independent	ر	کار	kā**r**	*work*

■ The letter zeh ز

The letter **zeh** ز is pronounced like the "z" in the English word "zoo," and has only two forms, final and independent.

In the previous chapter, we encountered a "z" sound in the letter **zal** ذ. In fact, there are still two other "z" sounds in the Farsi alphabet. More than a millennium ago, Farsi adapted the Arabic script. Later, many Arabic words found their way into spoken and written Farsi. Over time, Farsi speakers began to pronounce some of the Arabic letters in similar ways. Arabic speakers, however, pronounce these letters differently. The different letters that produce the sound "z" are examples of this. We will encounter more of these similar-sounding letters in upcoming chapters.

The following table shows the different forms of the letter **zeh** ز as it is used in words. Learn the letter, practice the pronunciation, and remember the meaning of each word.

Position	Form	As in	Pronounced	Meaning
Final	ـز	مزد	mo**z**d	*wage*
Independent	ز	بازار	bā**z**ār	*bazaar*

■ The letter zheh ژ

The letter **zheh** ژ sounds like the "g" in the French word "général," and has only two forms, final and independent. For convenience, we will use "zh" to denote the letter **zheh** ژ in our transcriptions throughout this book. The following table shows the different forms of the letter **zheh** ژ as it is used in words. Learn the letter, practice the pronunciation, and remember the meaning of each word.

Position	Form	As in	Pronounced	Meaning
Final	ـژ	مژه	mo**zh**eh	*eyelash*
Independent	ژ	ژاله	**zh**āleh	*dew*

Now practice writing the letter ر first, and then place a dot over it to convert it into ز. Next, add three dots to ر in order to make it into ژ.

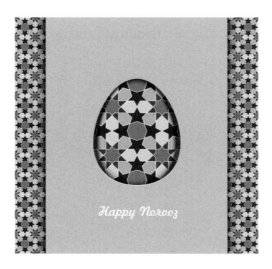

■ The letter kāf کـ

The letter **kāf** کـ is pronounced like the "c" in the English word "cat." The following table shows the different form of the letter **kāf** کـ as it is used in words. Learn the letter, practice the pronunciation, and remember the meaning of each word.

Position	Form	As in	Pronounced	Meaning
Initial	کـ	کم	kam	*little/low*
Medial	ـکـ	شکر	shekar	*sugar*
Final	ـک	نمک	namak	*salt*
Independent	ک	خوک	khook	*pig*

■ The letter gāf گـ

The letter **gāf** گـ is pronounced like the "g" in the English word "good." The following table shows the different forms of the letter **gāf** گـ as it is used in words. Learn the letter, practice the pronunciation, and remember the meaning of each word.

Position	Form	As in	Pronounced	Meaning
Initial	گـ	گاو	gāv	*cow*
Medial	ـگـ	جگر	jegar	*liver*
Final	ـگ	سگ	sag	*dog*
Independent	گ	مرگ	marg	*death*

Now practice writing the letter ک first, and then place an extra strike above the upper line to convert the ک into گ.

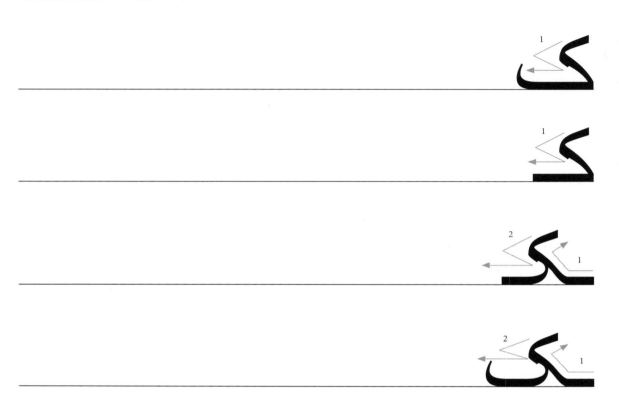

4.5 Let's Write

Now let's combine the letters we have learned in this chapter with the letters you learned previously to create new words. This time we omit the second column you saw in previous chapters, and you will have to join the letters by only having access to the independent forms of the letters. Two examples have been provided.

	Words	Letters in independent form
a.	کودک	ک و د ک
b.	مگر	م گ ر
c.		ژ ا ل ه

Words	Letters in independent form
d.	ک ا ر گ ر
e.	م ز ه
f.	گ ذ ا ر
g.	م ک ر
h.	ز ل ز ل ه
i.	ب ذ ر
j.	گ چ ک ا ر
k.	گ ه و ا ر ه

4.6 Cultural Insight: Spring and the Iranian New Year

Spring (**bahār** بهار) in Iranian *culture* (**farhang** فرهنگ) has a profound symbolic meaning. In fact, the Iranian New Year, called **Norouz**, نوروز (literally: "the new day") starts on the first day of بهار. New Year is celebrated for thirteen days, and four of these days are national holidays. A few days before the arrival of بهار, people dust and clean their entire *homes* (**khāneh** خانه) in a tradition called **khāne-takāni** خانه تکانی (literally: "to shake the home"). On the day of the spring equinox, families sit down around a decorated table called a **sofreh haftsin** سفره هفت سین (literally: "the seven S's table") to congratulate one another on the arrival of بهار. During the New Year's festival, people also visit their extended *family* (**fāmil** فامیل), starting from the oldest to the youngest, in a tradition called **dido bāzdid** دید و باز دید (literally: "visiting and revisiting"), to offer sweets and candies. On the thirteenth day of the نوروز, people celebrate the last day of نوروز, which is called **sizdeh-bedar** سیزده بدر (literally: "to see off the thirteen") by spending the day in *nature* (**tabiat** طبیعت).

 4.7 Vocabulary

[04sect7]

In this section, read the words in Farsi and memorize their meanings. Then play back the audio and check your pronunciation. You can use this section as a reference if you have a question about the meaning of the words in the Conversation section.

Transliteration	Farsi	Meaning
bāzār	بازار	*bazaar*
shāyad	شاید	*maybe*
behtar	بهتر	*better*
avval	اول	*first*
fāmil	فامیل	*family*
hafteh	هفته	*week*
tābestān	تابستان	*summer*
shomāl	شمال	*north*
khāleh	خاله	*aunt* (from mother side)
emshab	امشب	*tonight*
fasl	فصل	*season*

Transliteration	Farsi	Meaning
bahār	بهار	*spring*
kooh	کوه	*mountain*
Tochāl	توچال	*a mountain peak in Tehran*
Esfahān	اصفهان	*a city in central Iran*
Shirāz	شیراز	*a city in the south of Iran*
sobhāneh	صبحانه	*breakfast*
shahr	شهر	*city*

4.8 Grammar Point: Days of the Week, Months, and Seasons

The Iranian calendar is solar based, and consists of 365 days and 12 months. The week starts on Saturday, and Friday is a holiday. The first day of the each month usually falls on either the 20th or 21st of the Gregorian (i.e., Western) calendar. Practice reading the names of the days, months, and seasons in Farsi.

Days of the week

Transliteration	Farsi	Meaning
Shanbeh	شنبه	*Saturday*
Yekshanbeh	یکشنبه	*Sunday*
Doshanbeh	دوشنبه	*Monday*
Seshanbeh	سه شنبه	*Tuesday*
Chahārshanbeh	چهار شنبه	*Wednesday*
Panjshanbeh	پنج شنبه	*Thursday*
Jomeh	جمعه	*Friday*

Names of the months

Transliteration	Farsi	Meaning
Farvardin	فروردین	*March-April*
Ordibehesht	اردیبهشت	*April-May*
Khordād	خرداد	*May-June*
Tir	تیر	*June-July*
Mordād	مرداد	*July-August*
Shahrivar	شهریور	*August-September*
Mehr	مهر	*September-October*
Ābān	آبان	*October-November*
Āzar	آذر	*November-December*
Dey	دی	*December-January*
Bahman	بهمن	*January-February*
Esfand	اسفند	*February-March*

Names of the seasons

Transliteration	Farsi	Meaning
bahār	بهار	*spring*
tābestān	تابستان	*summer*
pāeez	پاییز	*fall*
zemestān	زمستان	*winter*

4.9 Song of the Day

[04sect9]

Iranian poetry and songs are filled with allegories of بهار, not only as a reference to the rejuvenation of the natural world, but also to the rejuvenation of the person. The following is a *poem* (**shear** شعر) about بهار which has been sung by some of Iran's most famous singers, such as Banān بنان and Zanganeh زنگنه.

ta bahāre delneshin āmadeh sooye chaman تا بهار دلنشین آمده سوی چمن
Since the pleasant spring has settled down on the grass
ey bahār ārezo bar saram sāyeh fekan ای بهار آرزو بر سرم سایه فکن
You, the spring of the desires, spread your shade on me
chon nasime nou-bahār bar āshiānam kon gozar
چون نسیم نو بهار بر آشیانم کن گذر
Like the breeze of a new spring, visit my little nest home
ta keh golbāran shaved kolbeyeh virāne man
تا که گلباران شود کلبه ویران من
So my desolate hut can become a sea of flowers

4.10 Exercises

1. Translate and write the following English words into Farsi.

    Example: week
    Answer : هفته

    a. _____ Spring

    b. _____ season

    c. _____ day

    d. _____ today

    e. _____ Friday

f. _____ mountain

g. _____ city

2. The following phrases consist of the words you have already studied in this chapter. Read them and then translate them into English.

Example: می‌خواهم ببینم

Answer : I want to see

a. _____ شاید باید برویم.

b. _____ خیلی دوستش دارم.

c. _____ فکر می کنم.

d. _____ امشب می پرسیم.

e. _____ بچّه ها میاند.

3. Complete the following table by writing in either the English or Farsi days of the week.

Thursday	
	شنبه
	سه شنبه
Monday	
Friday	
	چهارشنبه
	یک شنبه

4. Each of the following months falls during a specific season. Read the month and write down the name of the appropriate season in Farsi.

a. _____ بهمن

b. _____ آبان

c. _____ اردیبهشت

d. _____ مرداد

e. _____ تیر

f. _____ فروردین

g. _____ اسفند

Responses to writing practice in section 4.5:

Words

a. کودک

b. مگر

c. ژاله

d. کارگر

e. مزه

f. گذار

g. مکر

h. زلزله

i. بذر

j. گچکار

k. گهواره

Ādābeh sofreh

آداب سفره

Dinner Table Customs

In this chapter, we will learn five more new letters, and also study how to form imperatives in Farsi. The theme of this chapter is about dinner table customs, and giving and receiving souvenirs. As such we will discuss some of the expressions and formalities that people use on these occasions.

 **5.1 Conversation**

[05dia]

Soghāti سوغاتی **Soghāti**
Souvenirs

Nasrin's parents, Mrs. and Mr. Rahmati, have invited Nasrin, Daniel, and Sara for dinner. Mrs. Rahmati has also asked Nasrin's sister, Manijeh, and her family to join them at the dinner table. First, let's learn the Farsi names of the characters of the story. In the dialogue sections of this and the following chapters, the names of the characters are written only in Farsi (the names in English have been omitted intentionally). This is to encourage you to recognize Farsi words. Before starting to read the dialogues, make sure you can recognize these names in Farsi.

SĀRĀ سارا
DĀNIEL دانیل
NASRIN نسرین
MR. RAHMATI آقای رحمتی (**āghaye** Rahmati)
MRS. RAHMATI خانم رحمتی (**khānomeh** Rahmati)
MANIJEH منیژه
ĀZĀDEH آزاده
POOYĀ پویا

Now, listen to the conversation. Then replay the audio, this time reading along with the text.

Māmān khoreshtet kheili khoshmazeh shodeh*.

نسرین: مامان، خورشتت خیلی خوشمزه شده*.

Mom, your stew tastes wonderful.

Nooshe jān dokhtaram. Bāzam* bekesh.

خانم رحمتی: نوش جان دخترم. بازم* بکش.

Bon appétit my daughter. Have some more.

Āghāye Dāniel befarmāeed kabāb.

آقای رحمتی: آقای دانیال، بفرمایید کباب.

Mr. Daniel, help yourself to some kebab.

Merci pedar jān, kheili khordam.

دانیل: مرسی پدر جان، خیلی خوردم.

Thanks dear father, I've already eaten a lot.

Āzādeh jān be barādaret sālād bedeh.

منیژه: آزاده جان، به برادرت سالاد بده.

Dear Azadeh, give your brother some salad.

Pooyā, yek chizi bekhor.

آزاده: پویا، یک چیزی بخور.

Pooya, eat something.

Digeh* nemikhām*. Siir shodam.

پویا: دیگه* نمیخوام*. سیر شدم.

I don't want anymore. I am full.

Bad az shām

بعد از شام

After dinner

Yek chizhāye nāghābeli barātoon* āvordim*.

نسرین: یک چیزهای ناقابلی براتون* آوردیم*.

We have brought everyone some small gifts

Nemikhāst zahmat bekeshid.
You didn't have to trouble yourself.

منیژه: نمی خواست زحمت بکشید.

Māmān in lebās rā bepoosh.
Mom, please wear this dress.

نسرین: مامان، این لباس را بپوش.

Ghorboone* dastet, dokhtaram.
God bless you, my daughter. (Literally: "I die for your hands, my daughter.")

خانم رحمتی: قربون* دستت، دخترم.

**In dotā kādou ham barāye
Āzadeh va Pooyāand*.**
These two gifts are also for Azadeh and Pooya.

سارا: این دوتا کادوهم برای آزاده و پویا اند*.

Biāyeed. Begireed.
Come [you all]. Take [you all].

سارا: بیایید. بگیرید.

Merci Sārā Jān.
Thank you, dear Sara.

آزاده: مرسی سارا جان.

**Manijeh jān, yek kiif barāt*
āvordam*.**
Dear Manijeh, I have brought you a purse.

نسرین: منیژه جان، یک کیف برات* آوردم*.

Omidvāram ke doost dāshteh bāshi.
I hope that you like it.

نسرین: امیدوارم که دوست داشته باشی.

Dastet dard nakoneh*.
Thanks for troubling yourself. (Literally: "May your hand never ache.")

منیژه: دستت درد نکنه*

Beram* ājiil biāram* saremoon* garm besheh*.

خانم رحمتی: برم* آجیل بیارم* سرمون* گرم بشه*.

I will go to get some dried mixed nuts so we won't get bored. (Literally: "... bring dried mixed nuts so our head becomes busy.")

[05sect2]

5.2 Formal vs. Colloquial: Words from the Conversation

The colloquial forms of the words (محاوره ای **mohāverei**) in the Conversation have been marked with an asterisk (*). While reading the conversation, consider the context in which a colloquial word has been used. Then, study the formal forms (رسمی **rasmi**) to become familiar with the way you would address a person formally, or would find that word in a Farsi book or a newspaper.

Formal	رسمی	Colloquial*	محاوره ای *	Meaning
shodeh ast	شده است	shodeh	شده	*has become*
bāz ham	باز هم	bāzam	بازم	*again*
digar	دیگر	digeh	دیگه	*anymore*
nemikhāham	نمی خواهم	nemikhām	نمیخوام	*I don't want*
barāyetān	برایتان	barātoon	براتون	*for you (pl.)*
āvardehim	آورده ایم	āvordim	آوردیم	*we have brought*
ghorbān	قربان	ghorboon	قربون	*dear*
Āzādeh va Pooyā hastand	آزاده و پویا هستند	Āzādeh va Pooyā-and	آزاده و پویا اند	*They are Poya and Azadeh's.*
barāyat	برایت	barāt	برات	*for you (sing.)*
āvardeham	آورده ام	āvordam	آوردم	*I have brought*
dard nakonad	درد نکند	dard nakoneh	درد نکنه	*won't hurt*
beravam	بروم	beram	برم	*I go*
biāvaram	بیاورم	biāram	بیارم	*I bring*
saremān	سرمان	saremoon	سرمون	*our head*
beshavad	بشود	besheh	بشه	*become*

🎧 **5.3 Let's Talk**
[05sect3]

As we discussed in Chapter 2, **tārof** تعارف is an important feature of Iranian culture that is used to show respect and politeness toward others. تعارف is very often associated with specific words and expressions. This notion is especially more salient when giving orders or telling people what to do. For instance, in the conversation, when Mr. Rahmati wanted to tell Daniel to get more food, he said,

آقای دانیال بفرمایید کباب **Āghāye Dāniel befarmāeed kabāb**
(*Daniel, help yourself to some kabab*).

Other polite expressions include **khāhesh mikonam** خواهش می‌کنم (*I beg you or I ask you*), **lotfan** لطفاً (*please*), **Daste shomā dard nakoneh** دست شما درد نکنه (literally: "Your hand won't ache," said to show appreciation for someone's effort), and **Ghorboone dastetoon** دستتون قربون (literally: "I die for your hand," said to show appreciation, especially when receiving a gift).

Now let us practice some of these expressions. Read and repeat to yourself the following sentences. The words in shade are all polite expressions.

a. Befarmāeed **too.** بفرمایید تو.
    Please come on in.

b. Befarmāeed **injā beshinid.** بفرمایید اینجا بشینید.
    Please sit here.

c. Dastetoon dard nakoneh, **che ghazāye khoshmazieh!**
    دستتون درد نکنه چه غذای خوشمزیه!
    Your hand won't ache, what a great food it is!

d. Khāhesh mikonam, **tārof nakonid.** خواهش می‌کنم، تعارف نکنید.
    I beg you, don't make tarof (don't be polite).

e. Dastetoon dard nakoneh, **che mehmooni bāshekoohi!**
    دستتون درد نکنه، چه مهمونی باشکوهی!
    Your hand won't ache, what a magnificent party!

f. Ghorboone dastetoon, **mishe** lotfan **oon daro bebandid.**
    قربون دستتون، میشه لطفاً اون درو ببندید.
    I die for your hands, can you please shut the door.

5.4 The Letters *Beh, Peh, Teh, Seh, Noon,* and *Shin*

[05sect4]

Now we will learn six new letters which are frequently used in Farsi. The first four letters are very similar in form, and only differ in their number of dots and whether the dots are placed over or under the letter.

■ The letter beh ب

The letter **beh** ب is pronounced like the "b" in the English word "boy." The following table shows the different forms of the letter **beh** ب as it is used in words. Learn the letter, practice the pronunciation, and remember the meaning of each word.

Position	Form	As in	Pronounced	Meaning
Initial	بـ	بوس	boos	*kiss*
Medial	ـبـ	قبل	ghabl	*before*
Final	ـب	تب	tab	*fever*
Independent	ب	تاب	tāb	*swing*

■ The letter peh پ

The letter **peh** پ is pronounced like the "p" in the English word "pen." The following table shows the different forms of the letter **peh** پ as it is used in words. Learn the letter, practice the pronunciation, and remember the meaning of each word.

Position	Form	As in	Pronounced	Meaning
Initial	پـ	پر	par	*feather*
Medial	ـپـ	سپر	separ	*shield/bumper*
Final	ـپ	چپ	chap	*left*

Position	Form	As in	Pronounced	Meaning
Independent	پ	توپ	too**p**	*ball*

■ The letter teh ت

The letter **teh** ت is pronounced like the "t" in the English word "tree." The following table shows the different forms of the letter **teh** ت as it is used in words. Learn the letter, practice the pronunciation, and remember the meaning of each word.

Position	Form	As in	Pronounced	Meaning
Initial	تـ	تر	**t**ar	*wet*
Medial	ـتـ	بهتر	beh**t**ar	*better*
Final	ـت	سخت	sakh**t**	*hard*
Independent	ت	سوت	soo**t**	*whistle*

■ The letter seh ث

The letter **seh** ث is pronounced like the "s" in the English word "sand." As mentioned before, there are four different letters in Farsi with the sound of the letter "s." The following table shows the different forms of the letter **seh** ث as it is used in words. Learn the letter, practice the pronunciation, and remember the meaning of each word.

Position	Form	As in	Pronounced	Meaning
Initial	ثـ	ثروت	**s**ervat	*wealth*
Medial	ـثـ	کثیف	ka**s**if	*dirty*
Final	ـث	مکث	mak**s**	*pause*
Independent	ث	لوث	lo**s**	*tainted*

Now practice writing the four forms of the letter **beh** ب, and then write it again using a different placement of dots to form **peh** پ, **teh** ت, and finally **seh** ث .

■ The letter **noon** ن

The letter **noon** ن is pronounced like the "n" in the English word "nice." The following table shows the different forms of the letter **noon** ن as it is used in words. Learn the letter, practice the pronunciation, and remember the meaning of each word.

Position	Form	As in	Pronounced	Meaning
Initial	نـ	نمک	namak	salt
Medial	ـنـ	تند	tond	fast/spicy
Final	ـن	سن	sen	age
Independent	ن	جان	jān	life/dear

Now practice writing the four forms of the letter **noon** ن.

■ The letter shin ش

The letter **shin** ش is pronounced like the "sh" in the English word "short." For transliterations, we will use "sh" to denote the sound of the letter **shin** ش. The following table shows the four forms of the letter **shin** ش as it is used in words. Learn the letter, practice the pronunciation, and remember the meaning of each word.

Position	Form	As in	Pronounced	Meaning
Initial	ش	شیر	shir	*milk*
Medial	ش	جشن	jashn	*celebration*
Final	ش	ریش	rish	*beard*
Independent	ش	باش	bash	*be*

Now practice writing the four forms of the letter **shin** ش.

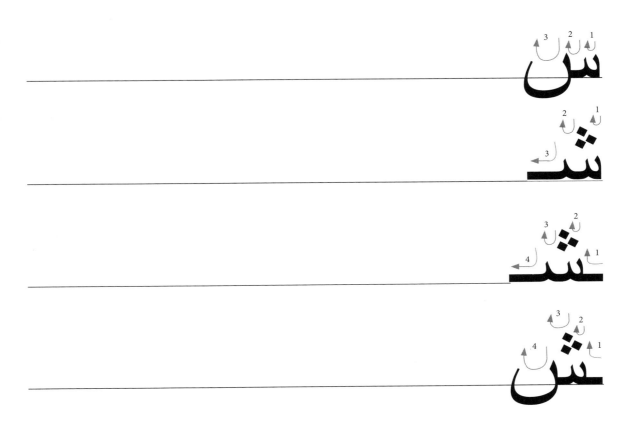

5.5 Let's Write

Now let's combine the letters we have learned in this chapter with the letters you learned previously to create new words. First you have to figure out what form each letter must take, based on its placement in a word, and then you have to join the letters accordingly. An example has been provided.

Words	Letters in independent form
a. شاد	د ا ش
b.	ر د ن ب
c.	ر د پ

Words	Letters in independent form
d.	ت ك ا س
e.	ث ل ث م
f.	م ا ن
g.	ت ش م
h.	ن ت س ش ن
i.	ت ب ا ث
j.	خ و س ن م
k.	ر ك ش ت

5.6 Cultural Insight

Sofreh سفره
Tablecloth

Iranian homes are usually carpeted with beautiful hand-woven Persian rugs, or **Farsh** فرش, and all rooms are cleaned and swept with a broom or a vacuum cleaner on the daily basis. Because of this, people take off their shoes when entering a home. Similarly, in traditional homes, most activities are performed on the carpeted floors rather than on the seats, sofas, and dinner tables.

During mealtime, a tablecloth, or **sofreh** سفره, is usually spread over the carpet, and family members sit down on the floor to consume *food* (**ghazā** غذا). On a typical Iranian سفره, other than the main meal, one can find fresh **noon** نون (*bread*; formal **nān**), **doogh** دوغ (*yogurt drink*), and a combination of fresh herbs such as *mint* (**nanā** نعنا), *basil* (**reyhān** ریحان), and *watercress* (**shāhi** شاهی). These herbs are called **sabzi khordan** سبزی خوردن (literally: "edible herbs"). Iranians enjoy *rice* (**berenj** برنج) with different kinds of *stews* (**khoresht** خورشت) as their main meal, depending on the region and ethnicity. *Skewered meat* (**kabāb** کباب) of all kinds is very popular and can be found on Iranian's سفره throughout the country.

سفره also signifies an important cultural and spiritual quality for Iranian people. Many traditions and practices are associated around the concept of سفره. For instance, سفره is considered the place of **barakat** برکت, the source of blessing or abundance. Children, for instance, are discouraged to jump over سفره, which is considered rude and disrespectful behavior. Occasionally, females give honor to *Islamic saints* (**emamzādeh** امام زاده) for a particular vow by throwing سفره for other women, usually neighbors and close relatives. In this tradition, special غذا or *pastry* (**shirini** شیرینی) is served on سفره accompanied by prayers.

5.7 Vocabulary

[05sect7]

In this section, read the words in Farsi and memorize their meanings. Then play back the audio and check your pronunciation. You can use this section as a reference if you have a question about the meaning of the words in the Conversation section.

Transliteration	Farsi	Meaning
khoresht/khorosht	خورشت	*stew*
khoshmazeh	خوشمزه	*delicious*
nooshe jān	نوش جان	*bon appétit*
bekesh	بکش	*serve/pull*
siir	سیر	*full/garlic*
shām	شام	*dinner*

Transliteration	Farsi	Meaning
nāghābel	ناقابل	*trivial/trifle*
zahmat	زحمت	*trouble/inconvenience*
lebās	لباس	*dress*
bepoosh	بپوش	*wear*
kādou	کادو	*gift*
kiif	کیف	*wallet or purse*
dard	درد	*pain*
ājiil	آجیل	*dried mixed nuts*
garm	گرم	*hot*

5.8 Grammar Point: Imperatives

Farsi infinitives add the ending -**dan** دن (and occasionally -**tan** تن) to the end of the verb, for instance, **khor**dan خوردن (*to eat*). An imperative is formed by removing -**dan** دن from the end of the verb, and by adding the letter "b" ب to its beginning. Therefore, the imperative of **khordan** is **b**ekhor بخور (*Eat!*). The plural of the imperative is created by adding -**id** ید to the end of the singular imperative form: **bekhor**id بخورید (*You all, eat!*).

In order to create the negative form of the imperative, we just replace the letter "b" ب with the letter "n" ن, for example **n**akhor نخور (*Don't eat!*), or **nakhorid** (*You all, don't eat!*). Some verbs are irregular.

 ## 5.9 Poem of the Day

[05sect9]

Omar Khayyam (1048–1131 AD) عمر خیّام

The Persian mathematician, astronomer, and philosopher, Omar Khayyām عمر خیّام is one of Iran's most popular poets. His **robāiāt** رباعیّات (*quatrains*) verses are famous for their celebration of the mundane aspects of life (although many people believe that the mundane language of his poetry is only a metaphor for very profound Sufi spiritual beliefs). The following is one of his **robāiāt** رباعیّات. First listen to the audio for pronunciation, and then try to understand the meaning of the words and expressions.

In yek do seh rooz nobate omr gozasht,

این یک دو سه روز نوبت عمر گذشت

These two and three days of life have passed by,

Choon āb be jooybār-o choon bād be dasht.

چون آب بجویبار و چون باد بدشت.

Like water passing through a stream and wind though a meadow.

Hargez ghame do rooz ma ra yād nagasht.

هرگز غم دو روز مرا یاد نگشت.

I never reminded myself of the sorrow of two days.

Roozi ke nayāmadast-o roozi ke gozasht.

روزیکه نیامدست و روزیکه گذشت.

The day that has not come yet, and the day that just went by.

5.10 Exercises

1. Convert the following Farsi infinitives into imperatives.

    Example: خواندن
    Answer: بخوان

    a. _____ خوردن

    b. _____ بردن

    c. _____ ماندن

    d. _____ رساندن

2. Draw lines to match the transliterations of the following Farsi words with the Farsi script.

tamāsha	تنها
shāneh	کاش
zendeh	تماشا
Masal	ابر
kāsh	شانه
tanhā	مثل
abr	زنده

3. The following Farsi imperative sentences have been written using transliterations. Rewrite them using Farsi script.

Example: **kabāb bekhor.**
Answer : کباب بخور

a. **Sālād biār.** _____

b. **Zahmat bekesh.** _____

c. **Lebās bepoosh.** _____

d. **Bāz kon.** _____

e. **Injā bemān.** _____

f. **Inrā bebar.** _____

4. In the top row of the table below, fill in the missing words from lines of the poetry you read in this chapter. In the second row, fill in your guess as to the English meaning of the words.

هرگز		دو		مرا	یاد نگشت
	sorrow		day		Not reminded

Responses to writing practice in section 5.5:

Words

a. شاد

b. بندر

c. پدر

d. ساکت

e. مثلث

f. نام

g. مشت

h. نشستن

i. ثابت

j. منسوخ

k. تشکر

Chapter **6** درس

Tejārat
تجارت
Commerce

In this chapter, you will be learning more Farsi letters, and you will also learn about shopping in Iran. You will also learn Farsi numbers as an important part of commerce.

6.1 Conversation

[06dia]

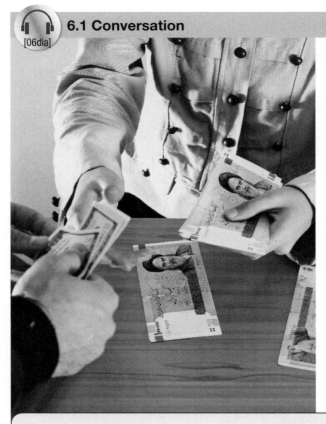

Dar bānk
در بانک
At the bank

Nasrin and Daniel need to stop at a bank and exchange some of their money into local currency. Listen to the conversation first. Then replay the audio, this time reading along with the text below.

bānkdār بانکدار
teller

Dāniel injā dame bānk beist.
Daniel, park close to the bank.

نسرین: دانیل، اینجا دم بانک بایست.

Chi* ehtiāj dāri?
What do you need?

دانیل: چی* احتیاج داری؟

Bāyad kami az poolemān rā tabdil konim.
We must change some of our money.

نسرین: باید کمی از پولمان را تبدیل کنیم.

Mitoonam* injā pārk konam*?
Can I park here?

دانیل: میتونم* اینجا پارک کنم*؟

Injā tavaghghof mamnooeh*.
Stopping is prohibited here.

نسرین: اینجا توقّف ممنوعه*.

Pas kojā beram*?
So, where can I park?

دانیال: پس کجا برم*؟

Yek kami jolotar pārkinge omoomi hast.
Further down, there's public parking.

نسرین: یک کمی جلوتر پارکینگ عمومی هست.

Dar bānk
At the bank

دربانک

Bāyad berim* bājeh moāmelāte arzi.
We must go to the currency exchange booth.

نسرین: باید بریم* باجه معاملات ارزی.

Bebakhshid āghā, mā mikhāhim dolār tabdil konim.
Excuse me, Sir. We want to exchange some dollars.

دانیل: ببخشید آقا، ما می خواهیم دلار تبدیل کنیم.

Nerkhe rooze dolār rooye tāblo ealām shodeh ast.
Today's dollar rate is shown on the display.

بانکدار: نرخ روز دلار روی تابلو اعلام شده است.

Hesāb konid, cheghadr ehtiāj dārid.
Calculate how much you need.

بانکدار: حساب کنید چقدر احتیاج دارید.

Mitavānim yek hesābe jāri ham bāz konim?
Can we open a checking account as well?

دانیال: می‌توانیم یک حساب جاری هم باز کنیم؟

Barāye che kāri ehtiāj dārid?
What do you need it for?

بانکدار: برای چه کاری احتیاج دارید؟

Mikhāhim poolemān rā dar ān negahdāri konim.
We want to keep some money in it.

دانیال: می‌خواهیم پولمان را در آن نگهداری کنیم.

Riāl ya dolār?
Rials or dollars?

بانکدار: ریال یا دلار؟

Riāl.
Rials.

دانیال: ریال

> **Pishnahād mikonam pasandāz bāz konid.**
> *I suggest you open a savings account.*
>
> بانکدار: پیشنهاد می‌کنم پس انداز باز کنید.
>
> **Bāsheh*, hamin kār rā mikonim.**
> *Ok, we'll do that.*
>
> دانیال: باشه* همین کار را می‌کنیم.

6.2 Formal vs. Colloquial: Words from the Conversation

[06sect2]

The colloquial forms of the words (محاوره ای **mohāverei**) in the Conversation have been marked with an asterisk (*). While reading the conversation, consider the context in which a colloquial word has been used. Then, study the formal forms (رسمی **rasmi**) to become familiar with the way you would address a person formally, or would find that word in a Farsi book or a newspaper.

Formal	رسمی	Colloquial*	محاوره ای *	Meaning
cheh	چه	chi	چی	*what*
mitavānam	می‌توانم	mitoonam	میتونم	*I can*
bekonam	بکنم	konam	کنم	*I do*
mamnoo ast	ممنوع است	mamnooeh	ممنوعه	*is prohibited*
beravam	بروم	beram	برم	*I go*
beravim	برویم	berim	بریم	*we go*
bāshad	باشد	bāsheh	باشه	*let it be*

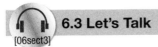 **6.3 Let's Talk**

[06sect3]

In the conversation, Daniel said to Nasrin,

Mitoonam injā park konam? میتونم٭ اینجا پارک کنم٭؟ (*Can I park here?*).

The first word in this sentence is the first person of the modal verb **tavānestan** توانستن (*can*). The following table shows the conjugation of this modal verb.

Transliteration (formal/informal)	Farsi (formal/informal)	English
mitavānam/mitoonam	می‌توانم\میتونم	*I can*
mitavāni/mitooni	می‌توانی\میتونی	*you can*
mitavānad/mitooneh	می‌تواند\میتونه	*he/she/it can*
mitavānim/mitoonim	می‌توانیم\میتونیم	*we can*
mitavānid/mitoonid	می‌توانید\میتونید	*you (pl.) can*
mitavānand/mitoonand	می‌توانند\میتونند	*they can*

Now let us practice making simple sentences using this modal. First read the transliteration aloud while paying attention to the meaning of the expression. Then practice reading the Farsi script. The words in shade show the different forms of **tavānestan** توانستن (*can*).

a. **Mitoonam beram?** (Formal: **Mitavānam beravam?**) میتونم برم؟
   Can I go?

b. **Mitoonid behem komak konid?** (Formal: **Mitavānid beman komak konid?**) میتونید بهم کمک کنید؟
   Can you help me?

c. **Nemitooneh biad injā.** (Formal: **Nemitavānd biāyad injā.**) نمیتونه بیاد اینجا.
   He/She/It cannot come here.

d. **Mitoonand be man begand.**
    (Formal: **Mitavānand be man begoyand.**) میتونند بمن بگند.
    They can tell me.

e. **Mitoonim behet telefon konim.**
    (Formal: **Mitavānim be to telefon konim.**) میتونیم بهت تلفن کنیم.
    We can call you.

f. **Mitoonid pisham bemonid?**
    (Formal: **Mitavānid pishe man bemānid?**) میتونید پیشم بمونید؟
    Can you stay with me? (Here, "*you*" can be taken as either the plural *you*, or the formal singular *you*.)

6.4 The Letters *Feh*, *Ghāf*, *Eyn*, *Gheyn*, and *Heh*

[06sect4]

Now we will learn five new Farsi letters. While reading and writing these letters, pay special attention whether a letter has a dot or dots, and if so where these are placed.

■ The letter feh ف

The letter **feh** ف is pronounced like the "f" in the English word "fan." The following table shows the different forms of the letter **feh** ف as it is used in words. Learn the letter, practice the pronunciation, and remember the meaning of each word.

Position	Form	As in	Pronounced	Meaning
Initial	فـ	فارسی	**F**ārsi	*Farsi*
Medial	ـفـ	هفت	ha**f**t	*seven*
Final	ـف	کف	ka**f**	*bubble/bottom*
Independent	ف	برف	bar**f**	*snow*

Now practice writing the four forms of the letter **feh** ف .

■ The letter ghāf ق

The letter **ghāf** ق is pronounced similarly to the French "r." The Conversation in this chapter (and also previous chapters) have many instances of the use of the letter **ghāf** ق , for example in the word **tavaghof** توقّف. Listen again to the audio of the Conversations and look for words containing this letter. Try to replicate the sound as closely as you can. The following table shows the different forms of the letter **ghāf** ق as it is used in words. Learn the letter, practice the pronunciation, and remember the meaning of each word.

Position	Form	As in	Pronounced	Meaning
Initial	قـ	قاضی	gh**ā**zi	*judge*
Medial	ـقـ	نقد	na**gh**d	*cash*
Final	ـق	عشق	esh**gh**	*love*
Independent	ق	بوق	boo**gh**	*horn*

Now practice writing the four forms of the letter **ghāf** ق.

■ The letter eyn ع

In Farsi, the letter **eyn** ع is pronounced like the letter آ ("a" as in "**a**pple" or "t**a**ll"), which we studied in Chapter 1. This letter is from Arabic, and is pronounced differently in that language. The following table shows the different forms of the letter **eyn** ع as it is used in words. Learn the letter, practice the pronunciation, and remember the meaning of each word.

Position	Form	As in	Pronounced	Meaning
Initial	عـ	علم	**a**elm	*science*
Medial	ـعـ	بعد	b**a**ed	*then/next*
Final	ـع	نفع	naf**a**	*profit*
Independent	ع	ابداع	ebdā**a**	*innovation*

◼ The letter gheyn غ

The letter **gheyn** غ is pronounced like ق (i.e., it sounds like the French "r"), which we just studied. The following table shows the different forms of the letter **gheyn** غ as it is used in words. Learn the letter, practice the pronunciation, and remember the meaning of each word.

Position	Form	As in	Pronounced	Meaning
Initial	غـ	غرب	gharb	west
Medial	ـغـ	بغل	baghal	embrace/side
Final	ـغ	جیغ	jigh	scream
Independent	غ	باغ	bāgh	garden

Now practice writing the four forms of the letter **eyn** ع, and then place one dot over the letter to convert **eyn** ع into **gheyn** غ.

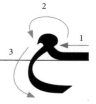

■ The letter heh ه

The letter **heh** ه is pronounced like the "h" in the English word "home," like the letter **heh** ح which we studied in Chapter 2. To avoid confusion, ح is called **heh jimi** جیمی ح, and ه is called **heh docheshm** چشم دو ه ("the **heh** with two eyes"). The following table shows the different form of the letter **heh** ه as it is used in words. Learn the letter, practice the pronunciation, and remember the meaning of each word.

Position	Form	As in	Pronounced	Meaning
Initial	ـه	هوا	ha**v**ā	*air*
Medial	ـهـ	بهار	ba**h**ār	*spring*
Final	ـه	مه	me**h**	*fog*
Independent	ه	ماه	mā**h**	*moon*

Now practice writing the four forms of the letter **heh** ه.

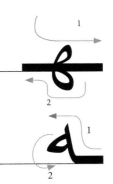

6.5 Let's Write

In previous chapters, we learned how to join letters to form Farsi words. In this chapter, we will take the bigger step of constructing simple phrases and sentences. As you have already learned the hardest part, making sentences should not be very difficult.

Farsi belongs to an Indo-European family of languages and, as such, its grammar is not that different than the English grammar. However, unlike English sentences which use the Subject-Verb-Object word order, formal sentences in Farsi use the Subject-Object-Verb word order. For example, in English we might say, "I bought a book." In this sentence, "I" is the subject, "bought" is the verb, and "book" is the object. In Farsi, the object and the verb are reversed, so we say, **Man yek ketāb kharidam** من یک کتاب خریدم (literally: "I a book bought").

Let us now write some simple sentences using Farsi words. In the following, you will see some Farsi words that have been mixed up. Rearrange them into grammatically correct sentences and write them out in Farsi.

Example:

گرفتند   هدیه   یک   بچه ها
Bachehā   yek   hedieh   gereftand
Children   one   gift   received.
Answer: بچه ها یک هدیه گرفتند.

Correct order

1.   خانه   خرید   آقای شکری
khāneh kharid āghāye shokri
bought   home   Mr. Shokri

_____

2.   پول   دادم   من
Man dādam pool
I   gave   money

_____

3.   علی   تماس گرفت   با من
Ali   tamās gereft   bā man
Ali   contacted   with me

_____

4.   شیراز   میریم   ما
Shirāz mirim mā
Shirza   go   we

_____

تخفیف گرفتن Takhfif Gereftan
Bargaining

Like people in many Middle Eastern countries, Iranians love to bargain, a cultural practice called **takhfif gereftan** تخفیف گرفتن. Shoppers negotiate for the price of almost all *goods* (**kālā** کالا). There are, however, some exceptions. For instance, the *price* (**gheymat** قیمت)

of *bread* (**nān** نان), *gasoline* (**benzin** بنزین), *tickets* (**belit** بلیط) (for buses, trains, events, etc.) and many other کالا and *services* (**khadamāt** خدمات) cannot be negotiated.

Store-owners are used to bargaining with their *customers* (**moshtari** مشتری), and have developed many skills to gently thwart their customer's plea to bring down the قیمت. For example, when a مشتری insists on a lower قیمت, the vendor may say, "**Ghābele shomāro nadāreh**" قابل شما رو نداره (literally: "It is not your worthwhile," which means that they may as well just take it as a gift). Of course, a مشتری is aware that such offers are only customary and are never intended to be taken literally. So, the مشتری may respond by saying, "**Sāhebesh ghābel dāreh**" صاحبش قابل داره (literally: "Its owner is worthy," which denotes that they would not take it from him for free). After a long exchange, the مشتری and the *vendor* (**forooshandeh** فروشنده) will finally reach an agreement for the قیمت of the کالا or خدمات.

 6.7 Vocabulary

[06sect7]

In this section, read the words in Farsi and memorize their meaning. Then play back the audio and check your pronunciation. You can use this section as a reference if you have a question about the meaning of the words in the Conversation section. Pay special attention to the new letters you learned in this chapter to make sure that you learn to pronounce them correctly.

Transliteration	Farsi	Meaning
beist	بایست	*stop/park/standup (imperative)*
ehtiāj	احتیاج	*need*
kami	کمی	*a little/some*
tabdil	تبدیل	*change/conversion*
tavaghof mamnoo	توقّف ممنوع	*no parking*
jolotar	جلوتر	*further down*
omoomi	عمومی	*public*

Transliteration	Farsi	Meaning
bājeh	باجه	*booth*
moāmelāte arzi	معاملات ارزی	*currency exchange*
nerkh	نرخ	*rate*
tāblo	تابلو	*display/sign*
ealām shodeh	اعلام شده	*has been announced*
hesāb konid	حساب کنید	*count/calculate* (imperative)
hesābe jari	حساب جاری	*checking account*
negahdāri	نگهداری	*keep/save/protect*
pishnahād	پیشنهاد	*suggestion*
hesābe pasandāz	حساب پس انداز	*savings account*

6.8 Grammar Point: Farsi Numbers

The following table shows the Farsi cardinal *numbers* (plural: **aadād** اعداد; singular: **adad** عدد). Read through these and practice the way they are written in Farsi.

Number in		Pronounced as	Written as
Farsi	English		
٠	0	sefr	صفر
١	1	yek	یک
٢	2	do	دو
٣	3	seh	سه
٤	4	chahār	چهار
٥	5	panj	پنج

| Number in | | Pronounced as | Written as |
Farsi	English		
٦	6	shish	شش
٧	7	haft	هفت
٨	8	hasht	هشت
٩	9	noh	نه
١٠	10	dah	ده
١١	11	yāzdah	یازده
١٢	12	davāzdah	دوازده
١٣	13	sizdah	سیزده
١٤	14	chahārdah	چهارده
١٥	15	pānzdah	پانزده
١٦	16	shānzdah	شانزده
١٧	17	hevdah	هفده
١٨	18	hejdeh	هجده
١٩	19	noozdah	نوزده
٢٠	20	bist	بیست
٢١	21	bist-o-yek	بیست و یک
٢٢	22	bist-o-do	بیست و دو
٢٣	23	bist-o-seh	بیست و سه
٢٤	24	bist-o-chahār	بیست وچهار
٢٥	25	bist-o-panj	بیست و پنج

| Number in | | Pronounced as | Written as |
Farsi	English		
٢٦	26	bist-o-shish	بیست و شش
٢٧	27	bisto-o-haft	بیست و هفت
٢٨	28	bisto-o-hasht	بیست و هشت
٢٩	29	bist-o-noh	بیست و نه
٣٠	30	si	سی
٤٠	40	chehel	چهل
٥٠	50	panjāh	پنجاه
٦٠	60	shast	شصت
٧٠	70	haftād	هفتاد
٨٠	80	hashtād	هشتاد
٩٠	90	navad	نود
١٠٠	100	sad	صد
١٠١	101	sad-o-yek	صد و یک
١١٠	110	sad-o-dah	صد و ده

6.9 Zarbol masal (Proverb) of the Day

[06sect9]

Ādame khoshhesāb sharike māle mardome.

آدم خوش حساب شریک مال مردمه.

The person who pays his /her debt on time,
is a partner to everyone's wealth.

Like the people in many traditional societies that lack modern credit institutions, Iranians for the most part must rely on someone's honor when engaging in *business* (**kasb** کسب) transactions such as delivery of *goods* (**kālā** کالا) or expecting *payment* (**vajh** وجه). Although in big cities such as Tehran, this honor may not be kept by some individuals, still most wholesale business transactions are still performed with personal credentials and verbal promises.

When initiating a business transaction, Iranians use the above proverb to remind one another of long-term benefits of honesty in *trade* (**tejārat** تجارت).

6.10 Exercises

1. Combine the following letters to make complete words.

    Example: م غ ا ز ه
    Answer : مغازه

    a. _____ ع ر و س

    b. _____ ق ا ن و ن

    c. _____ ت ا ب ع

    d. _____ م ه م

    e. _____ ب ا غ

    f. _____ ف ق ر

    g. _____ ق ه ق ه

2.   Using vocabulary from the Conversation, translate the following expression from English into Farsi.

a.   How much do you need?

_____

b.   This isn't a public parking.

_____

c.   We want to go further down.

_____

d.   Where has it been announced?

_____

3.   Look at the table of Farsi numbers (pages 118–120), and write the following numbers in Farsi.

Example : 32
Answer : ۳۲

a.   _____ 69   d.   _____ 40

b.   _____ 55   e.   _____ 198

c.   _____ 99

4.   How would you say the following in Farsi, if you were in a bank in Iran and speaking to a teller?

a.   I want to open a checking account.

_____

b.   What is the exchange rate for dollars?

_____

c.   What do you recommend, a checking account or a savings account?

_____

d. Where is the exchange currency booth?

_____

Responses to writing practice in section 6.5:

1. آقای شکری خانه خرید

2. من پول دادم

3. علی با من تماس گرفت

4. ما شیراز میریم

Chapter **7** درس

Ehsāsāt
احساسات
Emotions

In this chapter, you will learn the last four Farsi letters and two special diacritical marks. In the Grammar section, we will study how to make past tense sentences. Additionally, we will discuss some particular ways in which emotions are expressed in Iranian culture. Daniel is surprised to find out that mourners offer Halva, a pastry made of flour, sugar, rosewater, and saffron to people in the cemetery, in the memory of their dead ones.

🎧 7.1 Conversation
[07dia]

Ghabr mādarbozorg
قبر مادربزرگ
Grandmother's grave

The Paradise family has traveled to Mashhad مشهد, Iran's second largest city after the capital Tehran, where Nasrin visits the graveyard of her grandmother in **Beheshte Rezā** بهشت رضا cemetery.

Yādam miād* ke ghabresh dar ghateh chahār bood.

نسرین: یادم میاد* که قبرش در قطعه چهار بود.

I remember that her grave was in Section Four.

Cherā in khānoome dāreh* be hame halvā tārof mikoneh*?

دانیل: چرا این خانم داره* به همه حلوا تعارف میکنه*؟

Why is this lady offering halva to everyone?

Behesh migan* Nazri.

نسرین: بهش میگن* نذری.

They call it "Nazri" (a religious offering).

Rasm ast ke fāmilhāye nazik barāye mordegāneshoon* nazri bedan*.

نسرین: رسم است که فامیلهای نزدیک برای مردگانشون* نذری بدن*.

It's a custom for close relatives to offer "Nazri" to people in memory of their dead.

Bāyad hatman halvā bāsheh*?

دانیل: باید حتماً حلوا باشه*؟

Does it have to be halva?

Na, vali mamolan yā halvāst* yā shirini yā khormā, yā miveh.

نسرین: نه، ولی معمولاً یا حلواست* یا شیرینی یا خرما یا میوه.

No, but often it's halva, pastry, dates, or fruit.

Mibinam ke ādamhā sare ghabr khyli gerye o zāri mikonand.

دانیال: می‌بینم که آدمها سر قبر خیلی گریه و زاری می‌کنند.

I see that people cry and sob a lot at the graves.

Āreh, Irānihā khyli gham o ghosseh mordehāshoono* mikhorand.

نسرین: آره، ایرانیها خیلی غم و غصه مرده‌هاشونو* میخورند.

Yes, Iranians grieve and lament a lot for their dead ones.

Albateh, shāyad in benazar tazāhor biād*, vali vāgheiy ast.

نسرین: البته، شاید این بنظر تظاهر بیاد*، ولی واقعه ای است.

Of course, it may seem like pretend, but it's real.

Nasrin va Dāniel be didār marghad Emām Rezā miravand.

نسرین و دانیال به دیدار مرقد امام رضا میروند.

Nasrin and Daniel visit the mausoleum of Imam Reza.

Emām Rezā ki bood? Khyli marghad bāshokoohi dāreh*.

دانیال: امام رضا کی بود؟ خیلی مرقد با شکوهی داره*.

Who was Imam Reza? He has a magnificent mausoleum.

Emāme hashtome shiayān hast. Diin bishtare Irānihā shiia hast.

نسرین: امام هشتم شیعیان هست. دین بیشتر مردم ایران شیعه هست.

He is Shia's eighth Imam. Shia is the most popular Iranian religious group.

Agar che Irān khyli aghaliat hāye mazhabi dāreh*.

نسرین: اگرچه ایران خیلی اقلیّت های مذهبی داره*.

Iran also has many other minority religious groups.

Mesl chi*?

دانیال: مثل چی*؟

Such as?

Mesl sonni, masihi, kalimi, bahāi, va zartoshti.

نسرین: مثل سنّی، مسیحی، کلیمی، بهایی، و زرتشتی.

Such as Sunni, Christian, Jewish, Baha'i, and Zoroastrian.

Chera Emām Rezā dar Irān mordeh*?

دانیال: چرا امام رضا در ایران مرده*؟

Why did Imam Reza die in Iran?

Emām Rezā be dastoor khalifeh vaght be Khorāsān tabid shod.

نسرین: امام رضا به دستور خلیفه وقت به خراسان تبعید شد.

Imam Reza was exiled by the then caliph to Khorasan.

Bad ham dar deh Sannābād ke alān Mashhad shodeh* koshteh va dafn shod.

نسرین: بعد هم در ده سناباد که الان مشهد شده*، کشته و دفن شد.

Then he was killed and buried in the village of Sannabad, which now is called Mashhad.

 7.2 Formal vs. Colloquial: Words from the Conversation

[07sect2]

The colloquial forms of the words (محاوره ای **mohāverei**) in the Conversation have been marked with an asterisk (*). While reading the conversation, consider the context in which a colloquial word has been used. Then, study the formal forms (رسمی **rasmi**) to become familiar with the way you would address a person formally, or would find that word in a Farsi book or a newspaper.

Formal	رسمی	Colloquial*	محاوره ای *	Meaning
miāyad	می‌آید	miād	میاد	*he/she comes*
dārad	دارد	dāreh	داره	*he/she has*
mikonad	می‌کند	mikoneh	میکنه	*he/she does*
migoyand	می‌گویند	migan	میگن	*they say*
mordegāneshān	مردگانشان	mordegāneshoon	مردگانشون	*their dead's*
bedahand	بدهند	bedan	بدن	*they give*
bāshad	باشد	bāsheh	باشه	*to be*
halvā ast	حلوا است	havlāst	حلواست	*is halva*
mordehayeshān rā	مرده‌هایشان را	mordehāshoono	مرده‌هاشونو	*their dead's + ra*
benazar biāyad	بنظر بیاید	benazar biād	بنظر بیاد	*it appears*

Formal	رسمی	Colloquial*	محاوره ای*	Meaning
mordeh ast	مرده است	mordeh	مرده	*has died*
shodeh ast	شده است	shodeh	شده	*has become*

7.3 Let's Talk

[07sect3]

As you have seen throughout this book, the expression of emotion is a significant aspect of Iranian culture, and this is profoundly reflected in many languages spoken by the Iranian people, including Farsi. In the following, first we will introduce some common ways to express emotions, and explain their meanings. Then we will practice using these expressions. When practicing, first read the transliteration aloud while paying attention to the meaning of the expression. Then read the expression aloud again, using only the Farsi script.

a. **Vāstādan ghalb** واستادن قلب literally means "a standing-still heart" (**vāstādan** واستادن *to stand up* + **ghalb** قلب *heart*). These words refer to an experience of overwhelming emotion, which could be either happiness or fear.

Az khoshhāli nazdik bood ghalbam vāsteh. از خوشحالی نزدیک بود قلبم واسته.
From happiness, my heart almost stopped beating.

b. **Shoor zadan** شور زدن literally means "to hit salty" (**shoor** شور *salty* + **zadan** زدن *to hit*). These words refer to an experience of anxiety, when one is extremely worried about someone else who is not present.

Khyli delam shoor mizaneh. **Panj sāateh ke rafte biroon barnagashteh.**
خیلی دلم شور میزنه. پنج ساعته که رفته بیرون، برنگشته.
I am very anxious. He/she has left five hours ago and has not come back yet.

c. **Ābero bordan** آبرو بردن means to be disgraced by actions of others. **Ābro** آبرو means respect or honor, and **bordan** بردن means to carry, which is basically losing one's honor or respect.

Bachehām āberoomo **jolye mehmonā** bordand.
بچه هام آبرومو جلوی مهمونا بردند.
My children made me feel so ashamed in front of the guests.

d. **Del sokhtan** دل سوختن literally means "to have a burnt heart" (**del** دل *heart* or *stomach* + **sokhtan** سوختن *to burn*). These words signify that one is in such a state of empathy for another person that his or her heart is burning in pain.

Bichāreh, delam **barāsh** misoozeh. **Khyli tanhāst.**

بیچاره، دلم براش میسوزه. خیلی تنهاست.

Poor thing, I am so moved for him/her. He/she is so lonely.

e. **Khoon bejoosh āmadan** خون بجوش آمدن literally means "to have the blood boiled" (**khoon** خون *blood* + **joosh āmadan** جوش آمدن *to boil*). These words signify a situation in which a person is extremely furious and enraged with anger.

Anghadr aziat kard ke khoonam bejoosh āmad.

آنقدر اذیت کرد که خون بجوش آمد.

He/she bothered us so much that he/she brought my blood to the boiling point.

f. **To khod bodan** تو خود بودن literally means "being inside one's own body." The expression refers to a situation in which one is very withdrawn and pensive.

Khyli to khodeti. **Ye harfi bezan!**

خیلی تو خودتی، یه حرفی بزن!

You are so uptight. Say something!

 7.4 The Diacritical Marks *Tashdid* and *Tanvin*; and the Letters *Sād*, *Zād*, *Tā*, and *Zā*
[07sect4]

Now we will learn two Farsi diacritical marks which you might have encountered before. Additionally, we will learn the last four letters of the Farsi alphabet. These letters have an Arabic origin and are less frequently used in ordinary Farsi. However, it is essential to learn them in order to read and write Farsi fluently.

■ The diacritical mark tashdid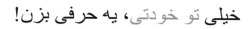

In Farsi, sometimes letters are repeated in a word. In such occasions, we write that letter only once, and then place a **tashdid** above it. This is done to remind the reader that that letter has to be pronounced twice or with emphasis. In this chapter you saw several instances of the **tashdid**. The following table shows how **tashdid** is used in some words. Learn the diacritical mark, and practice the pronunciation, and remember the meaning of each word. In the first column, you will see how a word would have looked like if it did not have a **tashdid**, and in the second column you will see the word the way it is actually written in Farsi.

Word without tashdid	Word with tashdid	Pronounced	Meaning
بچچه	بچّه	bachcheh	*child*
قصصه	قصّه	ghesseh	*story*
مضضر	مضّر	mozzer	*harmful*
امما	امّا	ammā	*but*

■ The diacritical mark tanvin أ

Some Farsi adverbs have an ending that consists of an **aleph** ‌ا with two strikes above it. The two strikes are called the **tanvin** أ. In Farsi, the **tanvin** is only used above the letter **aleph**, giving it the pronunciation of "an" like in the English word "artisan." In Arabic, the **tanvin** is used for other letters and has other functions. You have seen many instances of the **tanvin** in previous chapters, and may have wondered what it was. Now you know this diacritical mark, and how to pronounce it. The following table shows how **tanvin** is used in some words. Learn the diacritical mark, practice the pronunciation, and remember the meaning of each word. In the first column, you will see how a word would have looked like if it did not have a **tanvin**, and in the second column, you will see the word the way it is actually written in Farsi.

Word without tanvin	Word with tanvin	Pronounced	Meaning
ظاهرن	ظاهراً	zāheran	*apparently*
حتمن	حتماً	hatman	*certainly*
واقعن	واقعاً	vāghean	*really*
جددن	جدّاً	jeddan	*seriously*

Notice that the word **jeddan** جِدًّا has both a **tashdid** and a **tanvin**.

Occasionally writers omit or forget to place either a **tanvin** or a **tashdid** where they should be. However, as a reader, you need to recognize that a word has to have these diacritical marks and pronounce the words accordingly.

Now practice writing the diacritical marks **tashdid** and **tanvin** on the following lines.

■ The letter **sād** ص

In Farsi, the letter **sād** ص is pronounced like the "s" in the English word "sand." You may remember that we had two other letters, **sin** س and **se** ث, which have this same pronunciation. The following table shows the different forms of the letter **sād** ص as it is used in words. Learn the letter, practice the pronunciation, and remember the meaning of each word.

Position	Form	As in	Pronounced	Meaning
Initial	صـ	صبح	sobh	*morning*
Medial	ـصـ	قصّه	ghesseh	*story*
Final	ـص	نصّ	nas	*text*
Independent	ص	خاصّ	khās	*special*

■ The letter zād ض

The letter **zād** ض is pronounced like the "z" in the English word "zebra." Two other letters, **ze** ز and **zal** ذ , have already been introduced which have this same pronunciation, and you will soon learn yet one other letter which is pronounced with the "z" sound. The following table shows the different forms of the letter **zād** ض as it is used in words. Learn the letter, practice the pronunciation, and remember the meaning of each word.

Position	Form	As in	Pronounced	Meaning
Initial	ضـ	ضعيف	**z**aeef	*weak*
Medial	ـضـ	مضّر	mo**zz**er	*harmful*
Final	ـض	بغض	bogh**z**	*choked with sorrow*
Independent	ض	عوض	ava**z**	*change*

Now practice writing the four forms of the letter **sād** ص . Then add a dot above the letters to convert them into **zād**.

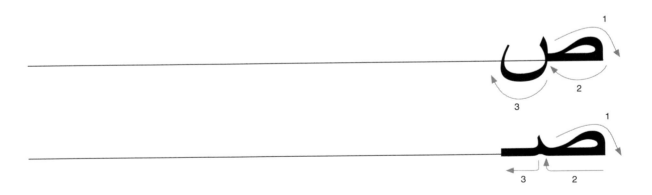

■ The letter tā ط

In Farsi, the letters **tā** ط and **te** ت have the same pronunciations, which is like the "t" in the word "Turkey." The following table shows the different forms of the letter **tā** ط as it is used in words. Learn the letter, practice the pronunciation, and remember the meaning of each word.

Position	Form	As in	Pronounced	Meaning
Initial	ط	عاطفه	**ā**tefeh	*affection*
Medial	ط	خطا	kha**t**ā	*error*
Final	ط	خط	kha**t**	*line/script*
Independent	ط	لاط	lā**t**	*rogue person*

Note: The word **lāt** لاط can also be written as لات.

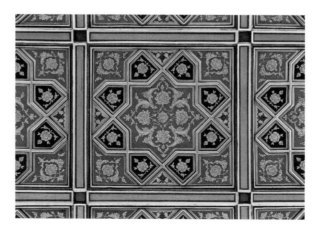

■ The letter zā ظ

The letter **zā** ظ is pronounced like the "z" in the English word "zoo," as are the letters **ze** ز , **zāl** ذ , and **zād** ض . Learn the letter, practice the pronunciation, and remember the meaning of each word.

Position	Form	As in	Pronounced	Meaning
Initial	ظـ	ظرف	**z**arf	*dish*
Medial	ـظـ	مظنون	ma**z**noon	*suspect*
Final	ـظ	حظّ	ha**z**	*delight*
Independent	ظ	لفّاظ	laffā**z**	*verbose*

Now practice writing the four forms of the letter **tā** ط , and then place one dot over the letters to convert them into **zā** ظ.

7.5 Let's Write

In the previous chapter, we wrote simple sentences by combining subjects, objects, and verbs. In this chapter, we will extend the writing practice by adding two more components—adjectives and adverbs.

Unlike in English, Farsi adjectives come after the noun they modify. For example, "a red ball" is written "the ball red," or **toope ghermez** توپ قرمز in Farsi (**tope** means *the ball* and **ghermez** means *red*). On the other hand, adverbs almost always come before the adjective they modify. Hence, we write:
besiār **khoob** خوب بسیار *very good*, khyli **ghashang** قشنگ خیلی *very beautiful*, and kāmelan **jadid** جدید کاملاً *totally new* or *brand new*.

Let us now write some simple sentences using Farsi words. In the following, you will see some Farsi words that have been mixed up. Rearrange them into grammatically correct sentences and write them out in Farsi. An example is given.

Example:

قشنگی	خریدند	لباس	آنها	خیلی
Ghashangi	**kharidand**	**lebās**	**ānhā**	**khyli**
Beautiful	*bought*	*dress*	*they*	*very*

Answer: آنها لباس خیلی قشنگی خریدند.

1. گران   هتل   است

است	هتل	گران
gerān	**hotel**	**ast**
expensive	*hotel*	*is*

_____

2. خیلی   است   بچّه   خوبی   او

خیلی	است	بچّه	خوبی	او
khyli	**ast**	**bach-cheh**	**khoobi**	**oo**
very	*is*	*child*	*good*	*he*

_____

3. جدید   خریدند   ماشین   کاملاً   آنها   یک

   jadid   kharidand   māchin   kāmelan   ānhā   yek

   new   *bought*   *car*   *totally*   *they*   *one*

---

4. غذای تو   است   خوشمزه   خیلی

   Ghazāye-to   **ast**   **khoshmazeh**   **khyli**

   your food   *is*   *tasty*   *very*

---

5. است   قدّش   کوتاه   خیلی

   ast   **ghaddesh**   **kootāh**   **kyli**

   is   *his/her height*   *short*   *very*

7.6 Cultural Insight

Āb o māb آب و ماب
Water and "Matter"

Farsi is filled with *poetry* (**shear** شعر). Farsi speakers change their speech using intonation, stress, and many forms of *repetition* (**tekrār** تکرار) in order to sound melodic. The poetry of speech in Farsi functions to influence listeners emotionally. Unlike many *Western traditions* (**rosoome gharbi** رسوم غربی), in which the label "emotional" usually carries a negative connotation, in Iranian culture, **ādame bā ehsās** آدم با احساس (*an emotional person*) is someone who has a superior way of viewing and interacting with the world.

Farsi speakers use many forms of تکرار and alliteration to achieve شعر in speech. For instance, it is very common to use several *adjectives* (singular **seffat** صفت; plural **seffāt** صفات) in tandem in one *sentence* (**jomleh** جمله), especially adjectives that have similar sounds or that rhyme. For example, in the Conversation section, Daniel used the words **geryeh o zāri** گریه و زاری (*cry and sob*) and Nasrin used the expression **gham o ghosseh** غم و غصّه (*grieve and lament*) to the same effect. Another common practice of Farsi speakers is the use of a *noun* (**esm** اسم) or صفّت and a similar-sounding token *word* (**loghat** لغت) next to it. This token word does not have any meaning at all. For example, in the phrase **āb o māb**, **āb** means water, but **māb** has absolutely no meaning at all. It is used merely to make the talk more melodic.

7.7 Vocabulary

[07sect7]

In this section, read the words in Farsi and memorize their meanings. Then play back the audio and check your pronunciation. You can use this section as a reference if you have a question about the meaning of the words in the Conversation section. Pay special attention to the new letters you learned in this chapter so that you learn to pronounce them correctly.

Transliteration	Farsi	Meaning
yādam miād	یادم میاد	I remember
ghabr	قبر	grave
ghateh	قطعه	section/piece/part
halvā	حلوا	a sweet made with flour
nazri	نذری	offering
rasm	رسم	custom
mamolan	معمولاً	usually
shirini	شیرینی	pastry
khormā	خرما	dates
miveh	میوه	fruit
gerye	گریه	cry
gham	غم	sadness/grieve
tazāhor	تظاهر	pretense
vāgheiy	واقعی	real
marghad	مرقد	mausoleum
hashtom	هشتم	eighth
Shia	شیعه	a branch of Islam

Transliteration	Farsi	Meaning
aghaliat	اقلیّت	*minority*
mazhab	مذهب	*religion*
Sonni	سنّی	*Sunni*
Masihi	مسیحی	*Christian*
Kalimi	کلیمی	*Jewish*
Bahāii	بهایی	*Baha'i*
Zartoshti	زرتشتی	*Zoroastrian*
Khorāsān	خراسان	*a province in Iran*
tabid	تبعید	*exile*
dafn shodan	دفن شدن	*to be buried*
deh	ده	*village*

7.8 Grammar Point

Zamāne gozashdeh زمان گذشته
The Past Tense

Farsi infinitives end in either **-dan** دن or **-tan** تن, for example **raft**an رفتن (*to go*) or **khor**dan خوردن (*to eat*). The simple past tense is constructed by dropping the **-an** of the infinitive, and by adding a personal pronoun ending. The six endings are as follows:

Singular pronouns		Plural pronouns	
-am (*I*)	م	**-im** (*we*)	یم
-i (*you sing.*)	ی	**-id** (*you pl.*)	ید
n/a (*he, she, it*)		**-and** (*they*)	ند

Note that the third person singular has no ending.

For example, for the past tense of the verb **raftan** رفتن (*to go*), first we drop the **-an** ن to form the root **raft** رفت. Then, we add an ending corresponding to the person of the verb.

raftam (*I went*)	رفتم	**raftim** (*we went*)	رفتیم
rafti (*you went [sing.]*)	رفتی	**raftid** (*you went [pl.]*)	رفتید
raft (*he/she/it went*)	رفت	**raftand** (*they went*)	رفتند

Similarly, we can turn the verb **khordan** خوردن (*to eat*) to the past tense by dropping the **-an** ن and adding personal endings as follows:

khordam (*I ate*)	خوردم	**khordim** (*we ate*)	خوردیم
khordi (*you ate [sing.]*)	خوردی	**khordid** (*you ate [pl.]*)	خوردید
khord (*he/she/it ate*)	خورد	**khordand** (*they ate*)	خوردند

 **7.9 Expression of the Day**

[07sect9]

"Elāhi bemiram" الهی بمیرم
"In God's name, I die"

In previous chapters, we talked how some Farsi expressions may seem like **exaggeration** (**eghrāgh** اغراق) to people in other cultures. The expression **elāhi bemiram** الهی بمیرم (*In God's name, I die*) is one of these.

For example, you can use this statement when seeing a relative's baby. On this occasion, saying **elāhi bemiram** الهی بمیرم or **elāhi bemiram barāt** الهی بمیرم برات (*In God's name, I die for you*) has an *endearing* (**aziz kardan** عزیز کردن) effect. You can also use this expression to show *sympathy* (**hamdardi** همدردی) when you see a friend or a child getting hurt. *Occasionally* (**gahgāh** گهگاه), you can even use it to show sincere *regret* (**taesof** تاسف) when you have caused emotional turmoil to someone you care about.

7.10 Exercises

1. Rewrite the following words using **tashdid**.

    Example: مجررد
    Answer : مجرّد

    a. _____ غصصه

    b. _____ نوواب

    c. _____ سرر

    d. _____ اتتفاق

    e. _____ قووت

2.   Rewrite the following words using **tanvin**.

Example: بعضن
Answer : بعضاً

a.   _____ لطفن

b.   _____ مثلن

c.   _____ تدریجن

d.   _____ اصلن

e.   _____ قاعدتن

3.   Name some of Iran's minority religious groups.

_____

4.   Convert the following verbs into the past tense, using all six of the personal endings.

Example: ماندن
Answer : ماندم ماندی ماند ماندیم ماندید ماندند

a.   _____   پوشیدن

b.   _____   درست کردن

c.   _____   بالا رفتن

d.   _____   بوسیدن

e.   _____   خاراندن

Responses to writing practice in section 7.5:

آنها لباس خیلی قشنگی خریدند.

1. هتل گران است.

2. او بچّه خیلی خوبی است.

3. آنها یک ماشین کاملاً جدید خریدند.

4. غذای تو خیلی خوشمزه است.

5. قدّش خیلی کوتاه است.

Answer Key

Chapter 1

1) 32

2) Initial, medial, final, and independent; س س ﺴ ﺲ

3) It literally means "my life, Daniel," but it has a similar meaning to the English "dear Daniel."

4)

5) a. سم **sam**   b. لم **lam**   c. لا **lā**   d. سال **sāl**   e. ملس **malas**   f. مال **māl**
   (Your transliterations may be somewhat different than those here. Don't worry about it now. Later you will learn that some of the short vowels in Farsi are not written but have to be guessed.)

6) Formal: **Chetor hastid?** Informal: **Chetori?**

7) a. **Mādar kojāst?** or **Mādar koo?**
   b. **mādar bozorg joon** or **mādar bozorg jān**
   c. **In Dānieleh?** or **In Dāniel hast?**
   d. **Dokhtaram Fārsi harf mizaneh** or **Dokhtaram Fārsi harf mizanad**
   e. **Dāniel o Sārā dārand miānd** or **Dāniel va Sārā dārand miāyand**

Chapter 2

1) او ، ما ، شما ، من ، تو

2) Singular **to** تو and plural **shomā** شما. **Shomā** شما is also commonly used as a polite form of "you" when addressing one person.

3)

4) a. **hāl**   b. **jesm**   c. **jām**   d. **kham**   e. **māl**
   f. **sāl**   g. **semej**   h. **khām**   i. **mokh**   j. **chāl**
   (Do not be disappointed if some of your responses are wrong. The purpose of this exercise is to make you aware of the fact that most short vowels in Farsi are not written but have to be guessed.)

Chapter 3

1) a. **dokhtaram**   b. **ham**   c. **yek**   d. **sar**   e. **hotel**
   (If some of your responses are wrong, do not be disappointed. The purpose of this exercise is to make you aware of the fact that most short vowels in Farsi are not written but have to be guessed.)

2) a. The long vowel is ی and the word is pronounced **hamin**.
   b. The long vowel is و and the word is pronounced as **joon**.
   c. The long vowel is ا and the word is pronounced as **tā**.
   d. The long vowel is ا and the word is pronounced as **kār**.
   e. The long vowel is ی and the word is pronounced as **chieh**.

3)

- a. زم
- b. جد
- c. خدا
- d. زال

4)

- a. When did you arrive?
- b. Where were you going?
- c. How are they coming?
- d. Why do you like it/him/her?

Chapter 4

1) a. بهار   b. فصل   c. روز   d. امروز   e. جمعه   f. کوه   g. شهر

2)

- a. Maybe we should go.
- b. I like it/him/her very much.
- c. I think.
- d. We will ask tonight.
- e. The children will come.

3)

Thursday	پنج شنبه
Saturday	شنبه
Tuesday	سه شنبه
Monday	دوشنبه
Friday	جمعه
Wednesday	چهارشنبه
Sunday	یک شنبه

4) a. زمستون   b. پاییز   c. بهار   d. تابستان   e. تابستان   f. بهار   g. زمستان

Chapter 5

1) a. بخور   b. ببر   c. بمان   d. برسان

2)

tamāsha — تنها
shāneh — کاش
zendeh — تماشا
masal — ابر
kāsh — شانه
tanhā — مثل
abr — زنده

3) a. سالاد بیار   b. زحمت بکش   c. لباس بپوش   d. باز کن   e. اینجا بمان
f. این را ببر

4)

یاد نگشت	مرا	روز	دو	غم	هرگز
Not reminded	to me (myself)	day	two	sorrow	never

Chapter 6

1) a. عروس   b. قانون   c. تابع   d. مهم   e. باغ   f. فقر   g. قهقهه

2)

a.   چقدر احتیاج دارید

b.   این پارکینگ عمومی نیست

c.   ما می خواهیم بریم یک کمی جلوتر

d.   کجا اعلام شده است؟

3) a. ۶۹   b. ۵۵   c. ۹۹   d. ۴۰   e. ۱۹۸

4)

a.   من می خواهم یک حساب جاری باز کنم

b.   نرخ تبدیل دلار چی هست؟

c.   چی پیشنهاد می کنید، یک حساب جاری و یا یک حساب پس انداز؟

d.   غرفه معاملات ارزی کجاست؟

Chapter 7

1) a. غصّه   b. نوّاب   c. سّر   d. اتّفاق   e. قوّت

2) a. لطفاً   b. مثلاً   c. تدریجاً   d. اصلاً   e. قاعدتاً

3) Sunni, Christian, Jewish, Baha'i, and Zoroastrian

سنّی، مسیحی، کلیمی، بهایی، و زرتشتی

4)

a.   پوشیدم، پوشیدی، پوشید پوشیدیم، پوشیدید، پوشیدند

b.   درست کردم، درست کردی، درست کرد، درست کردیم، درست کردید، درست کردند

c.   بالا رفتم، بالا رفتی، بالا رفت، بالا رفتیم، بالا رفتید، بالا رفتند

d.   بوسیدم، بوسیدی، بوسید بوسیدیم، بوسیدید، بوسیدند

e.   خاراندم، خاراندی، خاراند، خاراندیم، خاراندید، خاراندند

English-Farsi Glossary

A

affection **ātefeh** عاطفه

again **bāzham/dobāreh** بازهم\دوباره

age **sen** سن

air **havā** هوا

algorithm **algoritem** الگوریتم

analytics **tajzieh va tahlili** تجزیه و تحلیلی

anyway **behārhāl** بهرحال

apparently **zāheran** ظاهراً

aunt **khāleh/ammeh** خاله\عمّه

avatar **āvātar** آواتار

B

Baha'i **Bahāi** بهایی

bald **kachal** کچل

ball **toop** توپ

basil **reyhān** ریحان

bazaar **bāzār** بازار

beard **rish** ریش

beautiful **ghashangh/zibā** قشنگ\زیبا

before **ghabl** قبل

better **behtar** بهتر

blog **belāg** بلاگ

booth **ghorfeh** باجه

bottom **kaf** کف

B (continued)

boy **pesar** پسر

brand **nām-e tejāri/berand** نام تجاری\برند

bread **nān** نان

breakfast **sobhāneh** صبحانه

bubble **kaf** کف

business **kasb** کسب

but **ammā** امّا

C

car **machin/khodro** ماشین\خودرو

cash **naghd** نقد

certainly **hatman** حتماً

change **avaz** عوض

cheap **arzān** ارزان

child **bachcheh** بچّه

Christian **Masihi** مسیحی

city **shahr** شهر

comment **kāment** کامنت

computer **cāmpiuter/rāyāneh** کامپیوتر\رایانه

cow **gāv** گاو

crowdsourcing **jam sepāri/kerād sorsing** جمع سپاری\کرادسورسینگ

crown **tāj** تاج

cry **geryeh** گریه
culture **farhang** فرهنگ
customer **moshtari** مشتری

D

daddy **bābā** بابا
dates *(fruit)* **khormā** خرما
daughter **dokhtar** دختر
dawn **sahar** سحر
dear **joon/jān** جون\جان
death **marg** مرگ
delicious **khoshmazeh** خوشمزه
delight **haz** حظّ
description **sharh** شرح
dew **zhāleh** ژاله
difficult **sakht** سخت
dinner **shām** شام
direct **mostaghim** مستقیم
dirty **kasif** کثیف
dish **zarf** ظرف
dog **sag** سگ
door **dar** در
dress **lebās** لباس

E

early **zood** زود
easy **rāhat** راحت
ebook **ketāb-e elektroniki** کتاب الکترونیکی
embrace **baghal** بغل
emoji **imoji/sheklak** ایموجی \ شکلک
emotions **ehsāsāt** احساسات
empty **khāli** خالی

error **khatā** خطا
exile **tabid** تبعید
eye **cheshm** چشم
eyelash **mozheh** مژه

F

Facebook **Feysbook** فیس بوک
fairy **pari** پری
fall **pāeez** پاییز
family **fāmil** فامیل
fare **kerāyeh** کرایه
fast **tond** تند
father **pedar** پدر
fear **tars** ترس
feather **par** پر
festivity **jashn** جشن
fever **tab** تب
first **avval** اوّل
flower **gol** گل
fog **meh** مه
follower **donbāleh ro/faloer** دنباله رو\فالوئر
food **ghazā** غذا
for you **barāt/barāye to** برات\برای تو
Friday **Jomeh** جمعه
friend **doost** دوست
fruit **miveh** میوه

G

garden **bāgh** باغ
gasoline **benzin** بنزین
gift **kādou/hadieh** کادو\هدیه
give **dādan** دادن

god khodā خدا
good khoob خوب
goodbye khodāhafez خداحافظ
goods kālā کالا
grandmother mādar bozorg مادر بزرگ
grave ghabr قبر
grudge laj لج

H

hard sakht سخت
hardware sakht afzār سخت افزار
harmful mozzer مضرّ
hashtag hashtag هشتگ
he oo او
heart del/ghalb دل\قلب
hello salām سلام
help komak کمک
home khāneh خانه
horn shākh/boogh شاخ\بوق
hot dāgh داغ
hotel hotel هتل
how che-jori/che-goneh چه جوری\چگونه
how much cheh-ghadr چه قدر

I

I man من
innovation ebdāa ابداع
Instagram Instāgeram اینستاگرام
it ān ان

J

jar pārch پارچ

jasmine yās یاس
Jewish Kalimi کلیمی
judge ghāzi قاضی

K

kiss boos بوس

L

left (opp. of right) chap چپ
life zendegi/joon/jān زندگی\جون\جان
lips lab لب
little kami کمی
liver jegar جگر
love eshgh عشق

M

man mard مرد
maybe shāyad شاید
meme olgoye raftari/mim الگوی رفتاری\میم
milk shir شیر
mind zehn ذهن
minority aghaliat اقلّیت
mint nanā نعنا
miss someone del tang shodan دل تنگ شدن
mobile phone telefoneh hamrāh تلفن همراه
mom māmān/mādar مامان\مادر
Monday Doshanbeh دوشنبه
money pool پول
moon māh ماه
morning sobh صبح

mountain **kooh** کوه
Mr. **aghā** آقا
Mrs. **khānom** خانم
Muslim **Mosalmān** مسلمان
must **bāyad** باید

N

nail **mikh** میخ
nature **tabiat** طبیعت
need **ehtiāj** احتیاج
new **jadid** جدید
no **na** نه
north **shomāl** شمال
now **hālā/alān** حالا\الان

O

occasionally **gāhgāh** گاهگاه
offering **nazri** نذری
only **faghat** فقط

P

pain **dard** درد
part **ghateh/bakhsh** قطعه\بخش
passenger **mosāfer** مسافر
pastry **shirini** شیرینی
pause **maks** مکث
payment **vajh** وجه
person **ādam** آدم
pig **khook** خوک
place **jā** جا
plan **barnāmeh** برنامه
please **lotfan/befarmāeed** لطفاً\بفرمایید
podcast **pādcast** پادکست

poem **shear** شعر
price **gheymat** قیمت
probably **ehtemālan** احتمالاً
profit **nafea** نفع
public **omoomi** عمومی
purse **kif** کیف

R

rate **nerkh** نرخ
real **vāgheiy** واقعی
really **vāghean** واقعاً
red **ghermez** قرمز
religion **mazhab** مذهب
repetition **tekrar** تکرار
respect **ehterām** احترام
rice **berenj** برنج
rug **farsh** فرش

S

sadness **gham** غم
salt **namak** نمک
Saturday **Shanbeh** شنبه
savings account **hesābe pasandāz**
حساب پس انداز
science **elm** علم
scream **jigh** جیغ
search engine optimization
behineh sāzi motor-e jostojo
بهینه سازی موتور جستجو
season **fasl** فصل
seed **bazr** بذر
sense **hes** حسّ
sentence **jomleh** جمله

seriously **jeddan** جدّاً

services **khadamāt** خدمات

she **oo** او

shield **separ** سپر

side **baghal** بغل

sign **tablou** تابلو

sleep **khāb** خواب

snow **barf** برف

social media **resānehāye ejtemāii**
رسانه های اجتماعی

software **narm afzār** نرم افزار

some **kami** کم

son **pesar** پسر

speak **harf zadan** حرف زدن

special **khās** خاص

spring **bahār** بهار

stew **khoresht** خورشت

story **ghesseh** قصّه

sugar **shekar** شکر

suggestion **pishnahād** پیشنهاد

summer **tābestān** تابستان

Sunday **Yekshanbeh** یکشنبه

suspect **maznoon** مظنون

swing **tāb** تاب

sympathy **hamdardi** همدردی

T

tablecloth **sofreh** سفره

tag **tag** تگ

tainted **los** لوث

taxi **tāxi** تاکسی

thank you **motashakeram/merci**
متشکّرم\مرسی

that **ān** ان

then **baed** بعد

they **ānha** آنها

thirty **si** سی

this **in** این

thousand **hezār** هزار

Thursday **Panjshanbeh** پنجشنبه

ticket **belit** بلیط

tomorrow **fardā** فردا

tonight **emshab** امشب

totally **kāmelan** کاملاً

trade **tejārat** تجارت

traditions **rosoom** رسوم

trouble **zahmat** زحمت

Tuesday **Seshanbeh** سه شنبه

Twitter **Tooiter** توییتر

U

usually **mamolan** معمولاً

V

vendor **foroshandeh** فروشنده

very **khyli** خیلی

village **deh** ده

virtual **majāzi** مجازی

W

wage **mozd** مزد

we **mā** ما

weak **zaeef** ضعیف

wealth **servat** ثروت

Wednesday **Chahārshanbeh** چهارشنبه

week **hafteh** هفته

well **khoob** خوب

west **gharb** غرب

western **gharbi** غربی

wet **khis/tar** خیس\تر

what **che** چه

WhatsApp **Vātsap** واتس اپ

when **kay** کی

where **koo/kojāo** کو\کجا

whistle **soot** سوت

why **cherā** چرا

widget **vijet** ویجت

Wiki **Viki** ویکی

winter **zemestān** زمستان

word **loghat** لغت

work **kār** کار

worry **negarān** نگران

wrist **moch** مچ

Y

yes **baleh/āreh** بله\آره

you (formal) **shomā** شما

you (informal) **to** تو

Z

Zoroastrian **Zartoshti** زرتشتی

Farsi–English Glossary

ا

innovation **ebdāa** ابداع
respect **ehterām** احترام
probably **ehtemālan** احتمالاً
need **ehtiāj** احتیاج
emotions **ehsāsāt** احساسات
person/'adam' **ādam** آدم
cheap **arzān** ارزان
yes **āreh** آره
Mr. **aghā** آقا
minority **aghaliat** اقلّیت
now **alān** الان
algorithm **Algoritem** الگوریتم
meme **olgoye raftari/mim** الگوی رفتاری\میم
but **ammā** امّا
tonight **emshab** امشب
that/it **ān** آن
they **ānha** آنها
he/she/it **oo** او
avatar **āvātar** آواتار
first **avval** اوّل
emoji **imoji/sheklak** ایموجی\شکلک

this **in** این
Instagram **Instāgeram** اینستاگرام

ب

dad/father **bābā** بابا
bazaar **bāzār** بازار
again **bāzham** بازهم
garden **bāgh** باغ
must **bāyad** باید
child **bachcheh** بچّه
part **bakhsh** بخش
seed **bazr** بذر
for you **barāt/barāye to** برات\برای تو
snow **barf** برف
plan/program **barnāmeh** برنامه
rice **berenj** برنج
then/next **baed** بعد
embrace/side **baghal** بغل
please **befarmāeed** بفرمایید
blog **belāg/veblāg** بلاگ\وبلاگ
yes **baleh** بله
ticket **belit** بلیط
gasoline **benzin** بنزین

kiss **boos** بوس

horn **boogh** بوق

spring **bahār** بهار

Baha'i **Bahāi** بهایی

better **behtar** بهتر

anyway **beharhāl** بهرحال

search engine optimization

   behineh sāzi motor-e jostojo
   بهینه سازی موتور جستجو

پ

podcast **pādcast** پادکست

jar **pārch** پارچ

fall (autumn) **pāeez** پاییز

father **pedar** پدر

feather **par** پر

fairy **pari** پری

boy/son **pesar** پسر

Thursday **Panjshanbeh** پنجشنبه

money **pool** پول

suggestion/offer **pishnahād** پیشنهاد

ت

swing **tāb** تاب

summer **tābestān** تابستان

sign **tāblou** تابلو

crown **tāj** تاج

taxi **tāxi** تاکسی

fever **tab** تب

exile **tabiid** تبعید

trade **tejārat** تجارت

analytics **tajzieh va tahlili**
   تجزیه و تحلیلی

wet **tar** تر

fear **tars** ترس

repetition **tekrar** تکرار

tag **tag** تگ

mobile phone **telefoneh hamrāh**
   تلفن همراه

fast **tond** تند

you (informal) **to** تو

ball **toop** توپ

Twitter **Tooiter** توییتر

ث

wealth **servat** ثروت

ج

place **jā** جا

life/dear **jān** جان

seriously **jeddan** جدّاً

new **jadid** جدید

festivity **jashn** جشن

liver **jegar** جگر

crowdsourcing **jam sepāri/kerād sorsing**
   جمع سپاری\اکرادسورسینگ

Friday **Jomeh** جمعه

sentence **jomleh** جمله

life/dear **joon** جون

scream **jigh** جیغ

چ

left **chap** چپ

why **cherā** چرا

eye **cheshm** چشم

how **che-gooneh** چگونه

what **che** چه

Wednesday **Chahārshanbeh** چهارشنبه

how much **cheh-ghadr** چه قدر

how **che-joori** چه جوری

ح

now **hālā** حالا

certainly **hatman** حتماً

to speak **harf zadan** حرف زدن

sense **hes** حسّ

savings account **hesābe pasandāz**
حساب پس انداز

delight **haz** حظّ

خ

special **khās** خاصّ

aunt **khāleh** خاله

empty **khāli** خالی

Mrs. **khānom** خانم

house **khāneh** خانه

god **khodā** خدا

goodbye **khodāhafez** خداحافظ

services **khadamāt** خدمات

dates **khormā** خرما

error **khatā** خطا

sleep **khāb** خواب

good/well **khoob** خوب

car **khodro** خودرو

stew **khoresht** خورشت

delicious **khoshmazeh** خوشمزه

pig **khook** خوک

wet **khis** خیس

very/a lot **khyli** خیلی

د

to give **dādan** دادن

hot **dāgh** داغ

daughter/girl **dokhtar** دختر

door **dar** در

pain **dard** درد

heart/stomach **del** دل

follower **donbāleh ro/faloer**
دنباله رو\فالوئر

again **dobāreh** دوباره

friend **doost** دوست

Monday **Doshanbeh** دوشنبه

village **deh** ده

ذ

mind **zehn** ذهن

ر

easy **rāhat** راحت

computer **rāyāneh/cāmpiuter**
رایانه\کامپیوتر

social media **resānehāye ejtemāii**
رسانه های اجتماعی

traditions **rosoom** رسوم

basil **reyhān** ریحان

beard **rish** ریش

ز

trouble **zahmat** زحمت

Zoroastrian **Zartoshti** زرتشتی

winter **zemestān** زمستان

life **zendegi** زندگی

fast **zood** زود

beautiful **zibā** زیبا

ژ

dew **zhāleh** ژاله

س

shield **separ** سپر

dawn **sahar** سحر

difficult/hard **sakht** سخت

hardware **sakht afzār** سخت افزار

tablecloth **sofreh** سفره

dog **sag** سگ

hello **salām** سلام

age **sen** سن

whistle **soot** سوت

Tuesday **Seshanbeh** سه شنبه

thirty **si** سی

ش

horn **shākh** شاخ

dinner **shām** شام

maybe **shāyad** شاید

description **sharh** شرح

poem **shear** شعر

sugar **shekar** شکر

you **shomā** شما

north **shomāl** شمال

Saturday **Shanbeh** شنبه

city **shahr** شهر

milk/lion/faucet **shir** شیر

pastry **shirini** شیرینی

ص

morning **sobh** صبح

breakfast **sobhāneh** صبحانه

ض

weak **zaeef** ضعیف

ط

nature **tabiat** طبیعت

ظ

apparently **zāheran** ظاهراً

dish **zarf** ظرف

ع

affection **ātefeh** عاطفه

love **eshgh** عشق

science **elm** علم

public **omoomi** عمومی

aunt **ammeh** عمه

change **avaz** عوض

غ

food **ghazā** غذا

west **gharb** غرب

western **gharbi** غربی

sadness **gham** غم

ف

family **fāmil** فامیل

tomorrow **fardā** فردا

rug **farsh** فرش

vendor/seller **forooshandeh** فروشنده

culture **farhang** فرهنگ

season **fasl** فصل

only **faghat** فقط

Facebook **Feysbook** فیس بوک

ق

judge **ghāzi** قاضی

grave **ghabr** قبر

before **ghabl** قبل

red **ghermez** قرمز

beautiful **ghashangh** قشنگ

story/fable **ghesseh** قصّه

part **ghateh** قطعه

heart **ghalb** قلب

price **gheymat** قیمت

ک

gift **kādou** کادو

work **kār** کار

goods **kālā** کالا

computer **cāmpiuter/rāyāneh**
کامپیوتر/رایانه

totally **kāmelan** کاملاً

comment **kāment** کامنت

e-book **ketāb-e elektroniki**
کتاب الکترونیکی

dirty **kasif** کثیف

where **kojā** کجا

bald **kachal** کچل

fare **kerāyeh** کرایه

business **kasb** کسب

bottom/foam **kaf** کف

Jewish **Kalimi** کلیمی

little/some **kam/kami** کم\کمی

help **komak** کمک

where **koo** کو

mountain **kooh** کوه

when **kay** کی

purse/wallet **kif** کیف

گ

occasionally **gāhgāh** گاهگاه

cow **gāv** گاو

warm **garm** گرم

cry **geryeh** گریه

flower **gol** گل

ل

lips **lab** لب

dress **lebās** لباس

grudge **laj** لج

please **lotfan** لطفاً

word **loghat** لغت

tainted **los** لوث

م

we **mā** ما

mother **mādar** مادر

grandmother **mādar bozorg** مادر بزرگ

car **machin** ماشین

mom/mother **māmān** مامان

moon **māh** ماه

thank you **motashakeram** متشکّرم

virtual **majāzi** مجازی

wrist **moch** مچ

religion **mazhab** مذهب

man **mard** مرد

thank you **merci** مرسی

death **marg** مرگ

wage **mozd** مزد

eyelash **mozheh** مژه

passenger **mosāfer** مسافر

direct **mostaghim** مستقیم

Muslim **Mosalmān** مسلمان

Christian **Masihi** مسیحی

customer **moshtari** مشتری

harmful **mozzer** مضرّ

suspect **maznoon** مظنون

usually **mamolan** معمولاً

pause **maks** مکث

I **man** من

fog **meh** مه

nail **mikh** میخ

fruit **miveh** میوه

ن

brand **nām-e tejāri/berand** نام تجاری\برند

bread **nān** نان

offering **nazri** نذری

rate **nerkh** نرخ

software **narm afzār** نرم افزار

mint **nanā** نعنا

profit **nafea** نفع

cash **naghd** نقد

worry **negarān** نگران

salt **namak** نمک

no **na** نه

و

WhatsApp **Vātsap** واتس اپ

really **vāghean** واقعاً

real **vāgheiy** واقعی

payment **vajh** وجه

widget **vijet** ویجت

Wiki **Viki** ویکی

ه

hotel **hotel** هتل

gift **hadieh** هدیه

thousand **hezār** هزار

hashtag **hashtag** هشتگ

week **hafteh** هفته

sympathy **hamdardi** همدردی

air **havā** هوا

ی

jasmine **yās** یاس

Sunday **Yekshanbeh** یکشنبه

Photo Credits

All the photos in this book were taken by Donya Fazelnia and Majid Fazelnia, except for the following: Antonella865 | Dreamstime (pages 52, 73); Borna Mirahmadian | Dreamstime (page 134); Easyhwa | Dreamstime (page 123); Jelena Ivanovic | Dreamstime (page 56); Lublubachka | Dreamstime (page 76); Matyas Rehak | Dreamstime (pages 90, 139); Zaramira | Dreamstime (page 128)

Audio Tracklist

The Audio Recordings may also be Downloaded.

How to Download the Audio Recordings of this Book.
1. You must have an internet connection.
2. Type the URL below into to your web browser.

https://www.tuttlepublishing.com/farsi-persian-for-beginners-2

For support email us at info@tuttlepublishing.com.